The Peggy Nisbet Story

by Peggy Nisbet M.B.E.

Published By  HOBBY HOUSE PRESS, INC.
Cumberland, Maryland 21502

Additional Copies of this Book may be Purchased at $19.95
from
Hobby House Press, Inc.
900 Frederick Street
Cumberland, Maryland 21502
or from your favourite bookstore or dealer.
Please add $1.75 per copy for postage.

Printed in the United States of America
ISBN: 0-87588-299-4

Table of Contents

Preface 4

Introductory Letter 5

CHAPTER I   My First Doll - 1952 7

CHAPTER II   Starting a Doll Making Business - 1953 18

CHAPTER III   Early Development - 1950s 22

CHAPTER IV   Further Development - 1950s 28

CHAPTER V   Our First Workroom - 1950s 30

CHAPTER VI   Our First Trade Fair, U.K. - 1957 32

CHAPTER VII   Creation of the Peggy Nisbet Standard Doll - 1950s 35

CHAPTER VIII   Our First Factory - 1960s 39

CHAPTER IX   Scotland - 1950s-1984 44

CHAPTER X   British Exhibition - Coliseum, New York - June 1962
                 and Jetsell, U.S.A. - 1968 49

CHAPTER XI   Breaking into Export Markets - 1960s U.S.A., Canada,
                 Australia 52

CHAPTER XII   More Trade Fairs - 1960s, 1970s 65

CHAPTER XIII   The Fire - 1970 68

CHAPTER XIV   Rising from the Ashes - 1970 71

CHAPTER XV   Visits to U.S. Stores - 1975-1984 75

CHAPTER XVI   Soft Toys, Wooden Characters and 1in (3cm) Scale
                 Miniatures - 1975 83

CHAPTER XVII   Full Circle - Creation of Peggy Nisbet Bone China
                 Bisque Doll - 1976 97

CHAPTER XVIII   The Creation of a New Model 103

CHAPTER XIX   The Production of a Catalogue 107

CHAPTER XX   Specials 110

CHAPTER XXI   Museums, Doll Collectors and Visits to the Tower 110

CHAPTER XXII   U.F.D.C. and N.A.M.E. Conventions 131

CHAPTER XXIII   Doll Collecting in Great Britain 135

CHAPTER XXIV   The Silver Jubilee of Queen Elizabeth II - 1977 138

CHAPTER XXV   Family Album - 1909-1987 146

                 Epilogue 152

                 Catalogue Listings 153

Preface by Dorothy Coleman

Dolls have always been of great interest to the three Colemans and we were in London in 1968 when we first saw the Peggy Nisbet dolls. They were in Hamleys, our favourite toy store, as well as in other shops. These Nisbet dolls were made by a modern British doll maker who primarily produced portrait dolls and period costume dolls. When I returned to London with a group of doll collectors in 1970 I wanted to meet the maker of the Peggy Nisbet dolls, so Peggy was invited to have dinner with our group. She kindly accepted my invitation and thus began a close friendship that has lasted for many years. Unfortunately, our first meeting was only a short time after the dreadful fire that destroyed so much of Peggy's early work and records. This catastrophe was so recent at that time that I doubly appreciated Peggy's efforts to come to our dinner and meet strangers, even though they were doll collectors.

After our first meeting whenever I visited England or Peggy visited Washington, D.C., or we both attended one of the doll conventions in America, we always managed to see each other. Of course, dolls were the primary topic of conversation whenever we met. Peggy was interested in extending her work especially for collectors of dolls. At one of our dinners in Washington we discussed the possibility of making bisque head dolls. One time we discovered that my elder daughter, Elizabeth Ann, and Peggy's granddaughter, Charlotte, had gone to the same school in England.

Peggy Nisbet designed her dolls as well as being the producer of them. How often doll collectors have wished for firsthand information about the people who designed and produced the dolls that they collect! This is one reason why this Peggy Nisbet autobiography is of such special importance. In addition, this autobiography links her business with other well-known British doll makers of the past. Few doll makers in the past have provided any information at all about themselves or their products. Here, at last is the auto-biography of an artist who has designed countless dolls as well as supervising their manufacture. Peggy tells us how it all began and what her inspirations were that created a successful business.

Peggy Nisbet combed the markets to obtain just the right fabrics in which to dress her dolls. I have looked with awe at the multitude of rolls of cloth that were destined to form the Nisbet dolls' clothes. The texture, colours and designs all had to fit the special requirements of each type of doll. The trimming was also carefully selected as to size, shape and material. Special accessories required detailed study and design. Fortunately, nearly all of the Peggy Nisbet dolls came with a cardboard tag that identified the doll and the personage that the doll represented.

In 1977 I returned to England with another group of doll collectors and Peggy gave us a fascinating tour of her factory as well as entertaining the group in her charming home which is a converted water tower. All of the members of this tour group will no doubt read this autobiography of Peggy Nisbet with great interest. Each member of the group carried home a special Peggy Nisbet doll dressed as a "Somerset Farmer." The Nisbet dolls are made in the part of Somerset that since then has become the county of Avon. Avon includes Bath and other very picturesque parts of England.

Peggy has travelled around the world to find inspiration for her dolls. One year she visited Williamsburg, the colonial capital of Virginia, and made a series of dolls dressed in the period costumes of the Williamsburg era.

One of my favourite Peggy Nisbet dolls is the one representing the Garter King of Arms. The tabard, the scroll that this bisque doll carries, as well as the uniform, all make this a realistic representation of this special British herald. I asked Peggy if her Garter King of Arms represented any particular person but she said, "No, it was a general representation of the types that had served in this important office." The Garter King of Arms is head of the College of Heralds, where British titles are bestowed and verified. Slides of this colourful doll have been used many times when I am lecturing on British dolls.

The more we know about dolls, the greater is our appreciation of them. Thanks go to Peggy Nisbet not only for her dolls, but also for supplying information about them. Greater and greater emphasis is being placed on the impor-tance of knowing the provenance of dolls that are collected by both museums and individuals. Peggy Nisbet herself has supplied the documentation of her many dolls, thus ensuring that the correct information will be preserved for posterity.

Mrs. Dorothy S. Coleman

Introductory Letter

My intention, when I first planned to write a book about Peggy Nisbet dolls, was to make it a rather formal history of the company with events roughly in chronological order. Then one day, when going through and selecting photographs to include in the illustrated sections, I came across one taken with Susan Russell at The Meredith College of Continuing Education, Raleigh, North Carolina, U.S.A.

In 1982 I was invited by Dr. Sarah Lemmon, Executive Director, to be the guest speaker at their 2nd Doll Symposium to be held in June 1983. When I asked what kind of talk she would like me to give, she said that she had discussed the matter with her committee and their consensus was, and I quote, "We wish to hear about *you*: the source of ideas, how the research is done, how the ideas are then developed and dolls produced. We should enjoy anecdotes of your life and experiences in organising your company."

Obviously an ordinary lecture, illustrated with slides, was not what she wanted, so I went onto the platform with no notes and no photographs. A table had been placed alongside me upon which I arranged a group of my favourite models. For an hour I talked about my experiences in designing, making and selling dolls; then I asked if any members of the audience would like to come up, examine the dolls and ask for more information. There followed a most enjoyable time, with questions and answers following one another in quick succession. Everyone seemed to be enthralled with the anecdotes and personal reminiscences as much as with the main story. They wanted to know more about my home, the town in which I live, my family and the triumphs and disasters in the development of the business.

Instead, therefore, of writing a straightforward history of the company, I shall tell you a little about my family, my staff, customers, suppliers and colleagues. I have obtained photographs from many of them, so I hope to be able to present a picture of all those without whom there would be no Peggy Nisbet dolls to-day.

For those of my readers who make dolls themselves, I have described manufacturing processes; formulae for our own English bone china dolls and the unique procedure adopted for producing the moulds for our historical and character dolls for which we are, perhaps, most famous.

It is not the orthodox way of writing a book of this kind but neither was the way in which I developed the company. It has, however, been very enjoyable to write as though one was talking to one's friends, and I have derived enormous pleasure from sorting through old papers and photos, and re-living my experiences.

I hope you will enjoy the reading of the book as much as I have enjoyed the writing.

Peggy Nisbet M.B.E.

Peggy Nisbet with her daughter, Alison, and son, Peter, displaying her M.B.E. Medal (Member of The British Empire) which the Queen bestowed upon her for "Services to Export."

Dedication

To my husband Bill, Auntie Kitty and Alison

Acknowledgments

Amongst the many friends and colleagues who have assisted me in writing this book, I should like to acknowledge in particular the following, who have tolerated my whims and idiosyncracies with patience and good humour: Keith Pryke of Woodspring District Council, Leisure and Tourism Department; Jane Evans, Sharon Poole and Alec Coles of Woodspring Museum; John Loosley and Geoffrey Rye of the Avon County Library, Woodspring area; G. Baber of Barclays Bank; Faith Eaton; Caroline Goodfellow (Bethnal Green Museum); Jack Wilson, Mabel Perry, Malcolm Bowman, Dorothy Mantle and Maureen Hickling (House of Nisbet); Sue Worth, art work; Sylvia Bird; Pat Morton; Emily Wagstaff; Geraldine Lewis; Ken Poole; John Lewin; Graham Wiltshire and Cliff Atyco (photography), and also very many others to whom I say thank you. My daughter, Alison, and grandson, James, have helped considerably with their encouragement, criticism and advice.

My First Doll
—1952—

1952-1977 — The first 25 years of the reign of Her Majesty Queen Elizabeth II, was heralded as "The Second Elizabethan Era." It was in 1952 that I designed and dressed my first doll for sale commercially: a model of Queen Elizabeth in English china bisque, made to commemorate her coronation which was to take place the following year.

When deciding to write my book, it seemed appropriate that it should cover this period. Her Majesty celebrated her Silver Jubilee in 1977, and in the same year I celebrated my Silver Jubilee as a doll maker.

Princess Elizabeth came to the throne on the death of her father, George VI. She was a young married woman only 26 years old. She and her husband, Prince Philip, had one small son, Charles, and a daughter, Anne.

A wave of patriotism, enthusiasm and affection for the Girl-Queen swept the country. The second world war was over, and there was talk of the Second Elizabethan Era being one of prosperity and peace. A sense of optimism was abroad, and there was an upsurge of hope and expectancy. Everyone wanted to celebrate. Everyone wanted to do or make something to commemorate the occasion. My own wish was to make a model of the Queen for myself and fellow collectors. But how was I to go about it?

Thirty years ago rules governing any publicity in connection with the royal family were much more stringent than they are to-day. The approval of The Lord Chamberlain was necessary before any souvenir or replica of any member of the royal family could be made, and permission was not easily granted.

I decided to write to The Lord Chamberlain saying that I wanted to make a model of Her Majesty in coronation robes, and after several visits to his office in St. James's Palace, London, I was given permission to proceed.

The vision which had gradually become clearer in my mind, was to make a coronation doll in English bone china bisque, so that the hem of the skirt formed the base of the

Original 1952 model sketched by Peter Nisbet from memory 1983.

7

Original 1952 model (un-dressed) sketched by Sue Worth.

difficult to dress because of the rigidity of the arms, a problem which I had not foreseen when it was being modelled. As the arms were immoveable, the completed dress could not be put on the doll in the normal way, so one seam of the bodice had to be left open and stitched by hand on the outside, after the remainder of the gown was on the doll.

The costuming of the doll would have to be an inspired guess, because the design of the coronation dress would not be divulged until The Queen set out for the ceremony on Coronation Day, and the dolls would have to be ready before that day.

Then began a series of visits to public libraries, museums and portrait galleries, which has lasted until this day, since much of my research has been done in these establishments. On this occasion I looked at every illustration I could find of The Queen in evening dress, and came to the conclusion that she tended to wear traditional gowns with a round or boat-shaped neckline, a tight fitting bodice, and a full skirt hanging in graceful folds. It seemed likely that she would choose a gown of this type for her coronation, and it seemed almost certain that it would be embroidered or embellished in some way, but as it would be impossible for me to guess how, I chose a cream silk which would hang well on the small 7in (18cm) figure. I still had to feel my way by experimenting with various textures, weights and designs of cloth suitable for so small a model. I love the feel of different cloths and combinations of colours, and this has been one of the delights of my venture into doll making.

I put six panels into the skirt to give it fullness and yet retain a small waist. Underneath was an underskirt cut from the same pattern but in a thinner material, each panel being cut slightly smaller. The basic style of the dress that I had envisaged turned out to be very similar to the actual coronation dress, apart, of course, from the beautifully designed emblems embroidered on Sir Norman Hartnell's exquisite gown.

At The Tower of London where the coronation robes of previous monarchs were on display, every assistance was given to me to examine at close quarters the robes worn by The Queen's father, King George VI, and her grandfather, King George V. The Queen would undoubtedly wear a similar robe. Display cases were opened up for me, and I was able to walk round the models and examine the clothes from every angle.

There are so many colours of purple velvet on the market, and I wanted to make sure that I chose the correct shade of "royal purple." In addition to the colour, another problem was to find a velvet that was sufficiently light in weight to use on so small a figure. So many are stiff and thick, and I wanted a supple cloth which would give a flowing line, not a hard appearance. After much searching, success crowned my efforts, and we were able to start work on the prototype.

The second difficult task initially was to find a jeweller who could reproduce an Imperial State Crown, Orb and Sceptre with the limited finance at our disposal. In Weston-super-Mare we had, and still have, a small firm of manufacturing jewellers called C.G. Oxley & Co., whose owner, Mr. Pearson, took immense interest in our project and, after several attempts, he produced a simplified form of the crown formed by hand from fine rolled gold wire, into which were fitted some beautifully cut diamante stones to represent the balas-ruby known as the Black Prince's ruby, in the centre,

figure. I then wanted to dress this figure in a silk underskirt, a silk or brocade gown and the purple coronation robe. I aimed at making between 200 and 300, which was the maximum it seemed possible to achieve in the limited time available before the coronation ceremony.

Having discussed the proposed size with collector friends, I found that they favoured a doll 7in (18cm) high as being most suitable for a collection which could be easily displayed in or on fixtures in to-day's smaller rooms. There was no doubt as to the medium I would select in which to produce the model. Much of my time over the preceding years had been spent in visiting "The Potteries," which comprise the five linked towns of Stoke-on-Trent, Burslem, Hanley, Longton and Tunstall. Here it was that I had selected designs for Pountney & Co., the old Bristol Pottery which dated its history back to 1666, and claimed to be older than Wedgwood, although no dated piece has yet been found. So I wanted to make my doll in china bisque.

Whilst choosing designs for The Bristol Pottery as Design Consultant and Secretary to the Managing Director, Patrick Johnston, I had met a very talented modeller and potter from Stoke-on-Trent named Cyril Lancaster. I approached him to see if he would help me with the project because he had all the facilities for producing the figures on a commercial basis. For several months we worked closely together and when the first doll was cast, we were both delighted with the result.

This china bisque figure had fixed arms and was modelled complete with a full-skirted dress, the hemline, as I had envisaged, forming the base of the doll. It proved to be

Continued on page 17.

8

Writing my book at The Tower.

Entrance to The Tower.

Weston Bay from The Tower.

9

Vestments worn by H.M. Queen Elizabeth II at coronation ceremony, June 1953.

Detail of coronation dress material.

H.M. Queen Elizabeth II arriving at Westminster Abbey for her coronation, June 1953. Peggy Nisbet bone china bisque 8in (20cm) Tower Treasure model, designed in 1977 and shown with *King of Arms* (also Tower Treasure model).

P/624 *Prince Albert* and P/701 *Queen Victoria.* The Great
Exhibition, Crystal Palace, 1851.

P/611 *King Edward VII* and P/612 *Queen Alexandra.*

LEFT: P/709 *King George
V,* P/418 *H.R.H. Duke of
Windsor* (King Edward VIII)
as Governor of Bahamas and
P/710 *Queen Mary.*

BELOW: P/712 *King George
VI* and P/713 *Queen Eliza-
beth* (Consort of King
George VI).

Tower Treasure models, 1970s. Peggy Nibset bone china bisque. Left to right - Top row: *Arabella Stuart; Princess Elizabeth; Princess Margaret Rose;* Second row: *Queen Elizabeth The Queen Mother; Queen Mary The Queen Mother;* Third row: *Lady Jane Grey; Mary Tudor; Mary Queen of Scots;* Fourth row: *Queen Victoria (widow); Queen Elizabeth II; Prince Philip (Silver Jubilee); Queen Elizabeth I;* Fifth row: *King of Arms (Silver Jubilee); Queen Elizabeth II (coronation dress);* Sixth row: Coronation Chair (showing Stone of Scone); Coronation Vestments and Crown Jewels.

P/400 *H.M. Queen Elizabeth II in state robes (old model).*

P/400 *H.M. Queen Elizabeth II (current model) and P/416 H.R.H. Prince Philip (Admiral of The Fleet).*

LEFT: Silver Jubilee models: P/415 H.M. Queen Elizabeth II in formal evening dress and P/410 H.R.H. Prince Philip (Admiral of The Fleet).

BELOW: *Royal Page; Mistress of The Robes; Earl Marshall.*

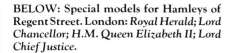

BELOW: Special models for Hamleys of Regent Street. London: *Royal Herald; Lord Chancellor; H.M. Queen Elizabeth II; Lord Chief Justice.*

P/417 *H.R.H. Princess Margaret* in wedding dress.

Captain Mark Phillips and *P/405 Princess Anne* in wedding dress.

P/789 Princess Victoria (wife of Kaiser Frederick III) and daughter of Queen Victoria in wedding dress.

Continued from page 8.

and some of the other famous jewels. The resultant crown was by no stretch of the imagination an exact replica of The Imperial State Crown, nor was it intended to be, but it was a very simple and effective copy made by a skilled craftsman, and well suited to the handmade doll I had designed. The orb and sceptre were easier, and similarly made with twisted rolled gold wire, the sceptre with a diamante and the orb with a rolled gold cross.

Finally, the prototype was ready and costumed, but how was I to sell the dolls? I had not the slightest idea how it should be marketed, but it was obvious that a handmade model of this kind would have to be sold through personal contact with the head buyer of whichever store or organization I decided to approach.

My thoughts at once flew to Harrods. I had met the china buyer previously, in connection with my Bristol Pottery activities, but although his department was a beautiful one, doll collectors, when buying in stores, tended to look in toy departments — so I asked my china buyer acquaintance to give me an introduction to his toy buyer colleague, Mr. Nicholson. Mr. Nicholson is now retired and I understand is living in Ireland, but I owe him a great debt of gratitude because he started me on my career.

Now, nearly 30 years later, Bob Marchant, his successor, is still selling the Peggy Nisbet range of dolls, and keeps a permanent display in his department, which is visited by customers from all over the world. We have made special models for Harrods, one of which is a doll of their famous doorman in his dark green uniform. Harrods themselves designed the gift box.

After I had made my appointment with Mr. Nicholson, I went to London with some trepidation, armed with my precious model. His first remarks were encouraging. He picked up the doll, turned it around and examined the materials and workmanship meticulously. Then he said, "How many are you going to make?" I told him that in the time available I could probably manage between 250 and 300. He said, still handling the doll, but not even looking at me, "Well, I'll take the lot, but only if you promise to make them exclusive to Harrods, and that you will guarantee to deliver them to the store by ....." and he gave me a date a few weeks before the coronation.

Can you imagine my excitement? I left the store treading on air.

Then began one of the many hectic periods which, for the next 25 years or more, were to become a way of life. First it was necessary to finance the project. Secondly, the dolls had to be moulded and thirdly, needlewomen had to be found who were meticulous in their work and reliable over their promises to complete it on time. Finally, sources of supply had to be found of materials for the clothes and robe, in sufficient quantities to make the stipulated number of models. For my prototype I had bought short lengths of cloth from local shops, but now larger quantities had to be purchased for immediate delivery: no easy task. Then there

were the crowns, orbs, sceptres, boxes, labels and packaging generally.

For finance I went to my bank and showed the manager the official order from Harrods, then asked him for a loan to cover the cost of materials and labour. This he granted and I was in business! I arranged for Cyril Lancaster to do the moulding and started upon the difficult task of finding expert needlewomen. This last job took much longer than I anticipated. Personal recommendations and replies to advertisements in newspapers produced plenty of applications but very few suitable seamstresses. I insisted upon each needlewoman making a complete set of clothes and returning them to me for inspection before being issued with any work. Many an experienced seamstress found herself unable to work on so small a scale, so the rejection figure was high. Two or three weeks elapsed before the final small, but elite group of highly skilled needlewomen was selected, but it was well worth the time and trouble. Engaging only the best was a wise policy long-term because the work was expertly done, making it possible for me to keep to my planned schedule, without sacrificing quality.

I was fortunate in that living with me was my elderly and dearly loved aunt, Kate Adams, a wonderful character, affectionately known to everyone as "Auntie Kitty." She was an exquisite needlewoman with a great sense of humour and infinite patience. She went through the process of cutting out and dressing their first doll with every seamstress I employed, either in my own home or in theirs, and this ultimately saved us much time, because we did not have to go through processes of trial and error, which would have been the case if we had left them to struggle on their own. She gave them confidence and inspired them to take pride in their work. This personal involvement has always been my first priority, and has continued throughout the years as the business grew.

The most difficult operation of all was the painting of the dolls' faces. After the prototype had been approved, a skilled artist had to be found. Finally, I discovered a lady artist who had previously worked in a pottery upon figurines. This was ideal because the painting of ceramics is a very specialised technique. This artist was the only one allowed to paint the faces, and I insisted that she should work with a portrait of The Queen always before her so that she could refer to it constantly. When painting a number of identical faces, one tends to get further and further away from the original with the result that the features alter. Therefore, she was only allowed to paint a specified number at each sitting to make sure that the likeness to Her Majesty was maintained.

The whole project was carried out from my own home. As I still had my commitment to The Bristol Pottery and travelled to Bristol every day, it was necessary to work on my dolls far into the night and the early hours of the morning, in addition, of course, to Saturdays and Sundays. It was chaotic and extremely hard work, but most exhilarating.

All the dolls were delivered to Harrods on time.

So ended my first business venture as a doll maker.

Starting A Doll Making Business

—1953—

Inspired by the small success of my first doll making venture, I began to give serious thought as to how I could develop a future business along similar lines.

In 1953 there were practically no small dolls dressed in British costumes on the market which visitors to the United Kingdom could buy to take home as souvenirs, either for themselves or to give to friends.

Whenever our family visited France, which we did regularly, our French friends always gave us dolls exquisitely dressed in the many beautiful regional costumes of the country. It seemed to me such a pity that we, with all our history and pageantry, had no dolls to depict our historical costumes and traditional uniforms, other than a few celluloid dolls with childish faces, ill-suited for the purpose. Those that were available were dressed inaccurately as guardsmen, pipers and beefeaters, in cheap fabrics and without any skilled needlework or authenticity.

Here then was the challenge I needed, so I decided to venture further into the world of doll making.

There appeared to be two interesting areas: first a collection of national costumes of different countries throughout the world; and secondly, historical costumes, in particular the beautiful and elaborate clothes worn by kings and queens throughout the ages and by the ladies and gentlemen of their courts. I decided to do both.

Understandably, the first national costumes I attempted were those of the British Isles. Here there was an immediate problem. Scotland, Wales and Ireland had what were accepted as their national costumes, but England had none. Scotland has the kilt, the tartans of the various clans and the bagpipes;

Ireland has a traditional country dress, usually consisting of a white blouse, green woollen skirt and woollen shawl or kerchief worn over the head, and the Welsh have their distinctive black chimney pot hats and traditional black, red and white wool flannels, but there is no English costume.

In Elizabethan times and onwards, country girls and maidservants wore simple dresses with pretty mob caps which varied in size and shape over the years. However, the dress itself remained basically the same, with a full skirt and tight bodice.

Frederick Wheatley, R.A., was born in London in 1747 and died in 1801. He specialised in portraits and domestic subjects, his first portrait being accepted for the Royal Academy in 1771. In the 18th century he did a series of paintings depicting street vendors of fruit, vegetables and household goods called "The Cries of London." His paintings became so popular and well-known that the dresses were acknowledged as being typical of the period. They were used in theatrical productions and historical pageants for years afterwards and are perpetuated on the stage and elsewhere to-day. Copies of the paintings are still amongst to-day's most popular prints in modern homes. I decided to use these costumes as my inspiration for a series of clothes for my English girls, and so "The Cries of London" series came into being. They have remained in every catalogue since my first range appeared and are still amongst the most popular of our models.

The first "Cries" to appear in a catalogue were BR 304 *Lavender Girl*, BR 305 *Nell Gwyn, Orange Seller*, and BR 306 *Cherry Ripe*, followed by three blank spaces against which

National costume dolls.

6in (15cm) *Happy* dolls.

Early models of "Cries of London," *Lavender Girl, Turnips & Carrots Ho!* and *Orange Seller.*

were the numbers BR 307, BR 308 and BR 309. Presumably I did this in order to advise collectors that three more "Cries" were to follow. In the next catalogue the second batch of three duly appeared as BR 307 *Turnips and Carrots Ho!*, BR 308 *Strawberries Sweet Strawberries*; and BR 309 *Flower Girl.*

The early model of the first strawberry seller was dressed in a very supple material which draped softly. It was most attractive. The colours, too, were muted, and similar to the original pictures.

Reproduced later in this book are two of my earliest catalogues, if lists so simple and amateurish can be graced with the name of catalogue. It was a very humble beginning, and a far cry from the sophisticated, illustrated and coloured catalogues we produce to-day. Nevertheless, I was very proud of these first efforts. In reproducing them in this book I look back and re-live the excitement of creating each model and printing the lists with their simple line drawings. The first catalogue bears the name "P.A. Nisbet & Son" and covers the period when my son, Peter, helped me to establish a business routine, and my husband, Bill, who was an accountant, dealt with banking, accounts and invoices, typing out the latter

with two fingers on an antiquated secondhand typewriter in the evenings in front of the fire.

The second catalogue, published a little later, had 77 models, an increase of 11 from the 66 on the first listing. By 1970 the range, which by then included soft toys, silkscreened B.B.C. characters, wooden nursery rhyme characters, souvenir dolls and Walt Disney characters, contained 206 items.

After making my decision to start a doll making business, I was enjoying myself researching and designing costumes and planning the ranges I wanted to make, but I had yet to produce the dolls on which to assemble the dresses. My ultimate ambition was to create my own Peggy Nisbet doll, but I knew that this would take a long time. Not only the size and type of doll had to be determined, but also the medium in which it could be produced. So I decided, as a temporary measure, to try to find a doll available on the market to experiment with my costumes and test the market. In this way I hoped to avoid making too many mistakes when creating and producing my own final doll.

I continued to experiment with cold setting resins, rubber solutions and plastics. In the fifties and sixties plastics were

19

Early model of *Strawberry Girl*.

still in their infancy, and small triumphs were followed by bitter disappointments as each effort had to be discarded for one reason or another. Still I persevered.

In the meantime I had found a pretty little doll on the market called *Rosebud*. These dolls were inexpensive, about 6in (15cm) tall, and although they had childish faces and bodies, they were well-proportioned and suitable for dressing in simple costumes. Moreover, they were on sale at the leading stores and easily available, so I bought a few with which to do some trials. Later, when larger quantities were required, I found out the name of the wholesalers from whom they could be obtained at a better price. Finally, in order to buy them at a still lower price, I made an appointment to visit the manufacturers at their factory and asked them to supply me direct.

I made an appointment with the Managing Director and upon being shown into his office, I noticed in a display cabinet, amongst all their undressed dolls, one which I had dressed and sold in my range of national costumes — I was surprised and pleased but did not have the courage to tell him that it was my work, because I still felt very much a newcomer in the doll world.

When my first small range of dressed *Rosebud* dolls was ready, I made a day trip to London and took them to the buyers at Harrods and Selfridges. Both placed sample orders. I was delighted.

The encouragement given to me by these two important buyers throughout the whole of my doll making career has been of enormous value. Without their guidance and constructive criticism, I would have found it much more difficult to enter the doll field. In particular, I have to thank "Pip" Loveland, who at that time was toy buyer at Selfridges. His advice over the years was invaluable. Whenever I produced a range of new models, he would look at them and give his opinion which was always helpful. I well remember the first time I called to see him. I was completely unknown and

"Pip" Loveland, buyer for Selfridges.

Rosebud dolls, 1953.

unimportant, with an untried, amateurish and new style of doll, but he greeted me with the greatest courtesy and spent the best part of an hour with me.

The first thing he did was to turn the doll upside down to see the underclothes, and he complimented me on the fact that they were all as well made as the top dresses. He told me that some manufacturers skimped with the underclothes! He then called in his secretary, Pauline Prestige, to see the range. Some years later Pauline herself became the toy buyer and she, too, has always been helpful with her advice. She was invariably outspoken with her criticism, but she was nearly always right and I respected her judgment. She became, and has remained, a good friend ever since.

After obtaining my order from Selfridges, I was naturally pleased to renew my association with Harrods later the same day. They had been pleased with the reception they received to my coronation doll and were ready to look at my new venture. The buyer gave me a sample order and I returned to Weston that night well pleased with my progress — two

orders from two of London's leading stores. It was a promising start.

These two sample orders were under £50 each, but to me they were worth a million dollars.

With the orders in my hands, I went again to see the manager of Barclays Bank, who this time opened the first small P.A. Nisbet & Son business account, the previous loan having been made through my personal account. As the business grew, Barclays continued to give me commerical advice as well as financial assistance until finally, a limited company, named Peggy Nisbet Limited was formed.

Now I had a business and would have to start production in earnest.

Recently, I was delighted to find a photograph of three of my early costumed *Rosebud* dolls. I do not have any of the dolls themselves and had no idea the photograph was in existence, so it was a joy to come across it. The centre doll is a *Peeress of the Realm*, and she has an *Elizabethan Lady of The Court* on either side.

Early Development
—1950s—

Production of my coronation doll had proceeded smoothly, although it was a continuous learning process. Now I had to learn how to make not only one, but several types of costumes simultaneously. I was offering customers a range of models so obviously when placing their first sample orders, the buyers wanted to try some of each. Therefore, they all had to be available.

Living with me, as I have mentioned in a previous chapter, was Auntie Kitty. Without her help and encouragement there would have been very few Peggy Nisbet dolls. This book is dedicated to her and to my daughter, Alison, who has been so involved in building the company, which she now runs with her husband, Jack Wilson.

Auntie Kitty's fiance, who was my mother's brother, died at the end of World War I. She came to stay with my mother for a short visit, but remained with my family until she died in 1979 at The Tower at the age of 95. She had helped my mother bring up my brother, sister and me, then devoted herself to my son, Peter, and daughter, Alison, and finally to my grandchildren.

Her whole life was spent doing things for other people and she was loved by all with whom she came in contact. She had a bubbling sense of humour, infinite patience and great strength of character.

When I started production, Auntie Kitty and I spent many hours together, cutting out paper patterns and making up the first prototypes of the costumes I had already researched and designed, and for which I had bought the materials. We started with just two needlewomen who worked in their own homes, both of whom had been engaged on my coronation doll. They were beautiful seamstresses who enjoyed doing the small, intricate work. One thing we discovered in the very early days was that not everyone who was good at general sewing was necessarily good at working on so small a scale. One exception was Christine Westlake, a trained tailoress. Christine started dressing our dolls in 1954 and is still working for us, over 30 years later. She has since told me that when making her first set of clothes (it was for *Mary Queen of Scots*), she found it so difficult to adapt to the small size of the clothes that she cried all night. Now she is one of our most prolific and reliable seamstresses. At the same time Gerda Slade and Julie McAulay joined our team of outworkers. They came to lunch with me recently at The Tower and I told them about this book and arranged for their photograph to be taken, which I have reproduced because I thought collectors might be interested in seeing them.

To obtain the best results we needed someone interested in the magic of doll making: someone with a great deal of

Peggy Nisbet at 7 Tower Walk with early models.

Group of early models with resin faces photographed in the dining room at 7 Tower Walk.

Peggy Nisbet with early outworkers. Left to right: Christine Westlake, Peggy Nisbet, Gerda Slade and Julie McAuley.

patience and a flair for producing a realistic effect. Applicants who just wanted to earn "pin money" when they were temporarily financially embarrassed were dissuaded from joining us, because involvement and a love of their work was essential for the production of a doll of character. Gradually I increased my little group of dedicated and skilled seamstresses until I had an expert team.

After interviewing a needlewoman who had been recommended to me, or who had answered an advertisement, an appointment would be made for her to come to the house when Auntie Kitty and I would go through the whole process of making the clothes and dressing a doll so that the seamstress would know exactly what to do. Then we would give her the dolls and patterns of the clothes, together with all the materials, threads and accessories plus, of course, a finished dressed doll as a sample. When she had completed her work we would either collect the finished dolls or, if she wished, she could come to the house to see us and discuss any point which needed clarification. It was a very personal relationship, resulting in a deep sense of involvement on her part. Consequently a well-made and unique range of character dolls came into being.

After a short while I employed two school leavers to work

with us as well. At this time the doll making was still being carried out in my own home, before we aspired to a factory.

Whilst busy obtaining orders, making the dolls to fulfil them, and expanding the business generally, I was, at the same time, energetically working on my main project, the development of a doll exclusive to Peggy Nisbet. I pursued every possible and sometimes impossible avenue, approaching large companies, individual craftsmen, laboratories experimenting in plastics and modern techniques and even dentists in case some of the moulding materials used for dentures could be adapted for my purpose.

The closest and most successful association I had was with Dean's Rag Book Co. I had first approached their design director, Richard Elliott, in 1954. He was then aged 84 but still actively involved with the company. I paid many visits to their modern factory at Merton, and they took enormous interest in my problem, experimenting for me in all kinds of media. Finally, they came up with a model made of latex, a rubberised material, and supplied me with small quantities of mouldings. It is only now, when writing this book, that I have appreciated just how good they were to me and how much time and money they must have spent in developing my doll, the cost of which could never have been covered by the price

23

they charged me. Dean's have a world-wide reputation for quality and upholding the highest traditions of the British Toy Industry, and well they deserve it. Their present directors, Ian Harry Scott and Michael John Crane, have become good friends over the years. Only recently Mike told me that when, as a young lad, he joined Dean's, of which his father was a director, one of his first jobs as a junior was to take a weekly supply of Peggy Nisbet dolls to London's Paddington Station, which was at the far side of the city from Merton, so that they could be put on a through train for special delivery to Weston-super-Mare. I have no example of this doll nor even a photograph and Mike says he has not been able to find one in their factories.

My association with Dean's had been a very important development from my point of view because other than my first bisque model, this was the first commercial doll I used which was made exclusively for me. It was another step towards attaining my ambition to have my own Peggy Nisbet doll on which to base my well-researched group of historical characters.

In Bristol I had been in touch with a very creative artist, John Lewin. After seeing examples of his work, I discussed with him my desire to produce a 7in (18cm) doll and my lack of success so far. John set about this task. He moulded some 7in (18cm) dolls using a new material which had been recommended to us by the laboratories of a large chemical company. The mouldings were excellent, the detail good, and they were easy to handle and paint. The arms were moulded separately, and during the moulding process small metal hooks were inserted in the arms near the shoulder on which a rubber band could be fixed to thread through the body. When these dolls were costumed, I was delighted with the result at the time, but inherent defects became apparent. The acid content of the resin attacked the elastic connecting the arms and also affected the dress materials, resulting in a disaster attached to our first export order with The Hudson's Bay Company of Canada.

This early version of the Peggy Nisbet doll was rather moon-faced and flat in features. I do not know if a doll now exists, but I have a photograph, reproduced herein, of one dressed as a Georgian Lady, and a few others showing the doll.

The early composition model was replaced some years later by our standard Peggy Nisbet doll, the development of which I have described in great detail. Many attempts and many disappointments were to take place before success was achieved.

On one of my sales trips I visited the London buying offices of The Hudson's Bay Company. I had shown the buyer, who was spending a few days in the U.K., a range of samples which had been prepared using our new doll. He placed orders for their stores in Montreal, Toronto, Calgary, Edmonton and others right across the country. It was my first export order and a great achievement: a break into the export market. When the order was completed, my husband and I packed it carefully in tea-chests and consigned them to their Canadian receiving depot.

We knew nothing about all the customs regulations and export invoice forms which had to be filled in, and were horrified by their complexity and the number of copies required, in some cases 14 or more of each! We visited Board of Trade offices and contacted any businesses we knew who exported their goods. Everyone was helpful. Finally the consignment was on its way.

A week or two later I was looking at a batch of *Lavender Girls*, which were standing on a shelf ready for labelling and thought that their dresses looked paler than usual. Upon examining them more closely, I was horrified to find that an actual change in colour was taking place. Worse was still to come. The metal hooks were turning green with verdigris and coming away from the body of the doll, so that the arms fell out. A chemical reaction had taken place in the mouldings due to the particular resin we had used! Production was, of course, stopped immediately and all the dolls destroyed.

Then came the difficult task of informing The Hudson's

John Lewin and members of the Shrubbery Doll Club.

Georgian Lady, circa 1959. Resin face.

National costumes dolls, circa 1959. Resin faces.

Elizabethan Lady, circa 1959. Resin face.

25

Early group, circa 1959. Resin faces.

Special resin model of King Henry VIII made for exhibition, 20in (51cm) high. Resin.

Bay Company about their order, of which I had been so proud. After a considerable amount of thought, I decided to cable them saying that a technical problem had arisen over the moulding of the dolls, and would they destroy the consignment upon arrival. This I presume they did. We re-made the order of several hundred models, using our old rubber type dolls. It was a severe blow, and very disheartening. Fortunately, this was the first order for which we had used the new dolls, so we were able to stop any more leaving the premises.

The Hudson's Bay Company waited for our replacement delivery and, despite the disastrous start to our business relationship, they became good customers and placed regular orders throughout the years to come.

From this small and not very propitious beginning our export business expanded by trade fairs and trade missions to the U.S.A. until some years later we estimated that over 70% of our production was sold overseas, and I had the honour in 1979 of being presented by H.M. The Queen with an M.B.E. (Member of the British Empire) Medal for Services to Export.

The immediate post-war years had made available to the small producer a variety of materials, resulting from wartime experiments in synthetics. Although "plastics" in various forms had been with us for some years, they were only produced under factory conditions. Among these were cassein (a milk by-product), bakelite (requiring heat and pressure), celluloid (a dangerous gun-cotton product), all highly inflammable and unsuitable.

Attempts to produce synthetic rubber in Germany produced Buna, and other substances related to this were vinyls and styrenes. These materials came onto the small consumer market and made possible the production of small scale moulds which were flexible, tough and durable. From these moulds cold-setting resin objects could be cast.

As has just been described, early attempts to produce dolls from these resins appeared at first to be satisfactory, but during the dressing stage serious problems arose. The resin, supplied as a syrup, required the addition of a hardener to solidify it. The chemical of which the hardener consisted quite soon affected the dyes of the dresses, also the rubber bands connecting the dolls' arms. Further experiments ensued, with still more disappointing results.

Obviously, some other method of making dolls had to be found. Injection moulded plastics were springing up in all directions. Once molecular structures were mastered, manufacturers were able to produce mouldings ranging from flexible toys to rigid fittings and fixtures in all colours and sizes. Among these materials was high impact polystyrene: tough and rigid, it proved to be an ideal substance for producing our dolls in the quantity we required.

The development of this technique is described in the next chapter. It was a turning point in the growth of the company, and when our first styrene dolls were in production, the business surged ahead.

Injection moulding of a 7in (18cm) doll had to be done in a factory with heavy machinery, so John Lewin obviously could not do them, but the demand for accessories for our dolls increased as our range grew until it became almost a business in its own right. Many of these were made of rubber (cast latex) and some were vacuum formed from acetate sheet. All these had to be modelled and moulds made for production. They were sprayed and hand-painted in materials that were non-toxic and durable. John did them all and delivered them to Weston once a week.

Inevitably, moments of panic occurred, such as forthcoming royal weddings, the emergence of a highly topical character or a surge of demand for one particular subject.

Much research had to be done to ensure accuracy. On one occasion a visit was made to the Royal Marine barracks in Bristol in order to examine the bandsmen's helmets, drums and sticks. The commanding officer was very helpful, and interested enough to offer to send two bandsmen to Weston in full equipment: a bass drummer in his leopard skin surcoat, and a trumpeter, for first-hand examination of uniforms and accoutrements.

There is a story attached to this. My housekeeper, Emily Wagstaff, had a neighbour with a nine-year-old son. She gave him one of our *Royal Marine Drummers* as a Christmas present. So delighted was the young boy with his drummer-doll that he decided then and there that when he grew up, he would become a drummer in the Royal Marines; that is exactly what he did!

A list of the accessories John made would fill pages. They included a Balinese dancer's headdress, mediaeval wimples, Dutch sabots, jockey caps, guardsmen's helmets and breast-plates, Mounties' holsters, cairngorm brooches, bagpipes and sporrans.

Various devices to ensure standardization were developed: jigs, formers, cutters, punches, presses and a variety of implements were made — one of the most ingenious ideas was the production of metal punches to make skates for the little 6in (15cm) *Ballerina* doll which began a whole series of cutters for use in a press for various items.

Early model of *Queen Elizabeth I*.

Early *Scottish Piper* with resin face.

27

CHAPTER IV

Further Development
—————— 1950s ——————

The business was now growing steadily. It could no longer be run from the house, but as yet I had not found suitable premises which we could afford.

For some time we had been using an old, disused water tower, which was situated a few doors away from my home. This was rented from the local council which had been using it for the storage of garden implements. The council allowed us to rent the building for the purpose of storing our materials and boxes. We also used the ground floor as our packing department.

One room at the top had a magnificent view over the Mendip Hills and the Bristol Channel. This we kept as a work-room. Here my husband, Auntie Kitty and I would gather together the work returned by our outworkers in order to get it ready for packing. The three of us had a small belt-line system going. Auntie Kitty would check every dressed doll and pass it to me. I would make the hair-style from finely plaited mohair and sew on any accessories, then pass it to Bill who would write the name and number of the doll and attach the label to the appropriate wrist. There was no lighting installed in The Tower at that time, so I bought some miniature oil lamps at Woolworths, about 6in (15cm) or 7in (18cm) high, and each of us had two lamps in front of us. I do not suppose this was particularly good for our eyesight, but it was adequate for our purpose.

There was no form of heating either, so we bought an oil heater, and as the weather got cooler, we huddled over its warmth. One episode remains very clear in my mind. We were working on an order which had to be completed and it was 3 or 4 o'clock in the morning before we finished. When, with our torches in our hands, we opened The Tower door, we found there had been a fall of snow. I was just negotiating the steps which led from The Tower to the road when I slipped on the ice and went sprawling onto the path beneath. I was not hurt, but disgruntled because I was so tired and had to catch the 7:45 a.m. train to the Bristol Pottery in three hours time. It was only just possible to have a bath and breakfast. It would have been fatal to go to bed. When I returned from Bristol that evening, the order had been packed and despatched and we treated ourselves to a night off!

So much of our early development revolved round The Tower that I am very attached to the building. Many years later, after my husband's death and when the business was established in a new factory, I sold my house and with the proceeds built an extension onto The Tower, which is now my home, where many of my readers will have visited me and will, I hope, continue to arrive.

We were still expanding and it was now imperative to have room for clerical staff as well as for manufacturing space. A basement flat, consisting of several rooms, became vacant near my home and, at the same time, we heard of a small work-room in the centre of the town which had become empty. Neither of the premises would have been of any use on its own, but together they were a possible temporary solution so we took them both. I continued to keep my eyes open for a suitable work-room or small factory, but I wanted to buy rather than rent, and our resources were not yet sufficient to embark upon such a large outlay. The rooms in the flat we used as offices and the small work-room became the manufacturing unit for our sailor dolls.

By this time my son, Peter, who had left college and completed his military service, found that his own little business was growing so rapidly that he could no longer spend so much time helping me with the dolls. Bill and I had bought him a small practice from a retiring agent who had represented The Bristol Pottery and who was very well respected in the trade. He sold dinnerware, glassware and cutlery to hotels and restaurants. Peter bought himself a small van, fitted it out himself as a travelling showroom, and was building up a sound little business for himself. His company, Peter Nisbet & Company Limited, is now one of the leading businesses of its kind in the country, designing and equipping restaurants, kitchens and canteens for large hotel groups, hospitals and factories.

My husband, an accountant, had been helping me, particularly with the accounts but he also had his own job to do, so I needed staff.

One day we were discussing the problem with an old family friend, Clifton Smith-Cox, whose mother had been my mother's bridesmaid. Clifton was very interested in the potential of the doll business and we discussed its possible growth. He said to me, and I clearly remember his exact words: "If you are going to continue you will need to form a Limited Company." He then added, and these are the words I remember so well: "If you are prepared to go into this business seriously, and not just treat it as a hobby, I will help you to form the company and to get it operative."

A company was formed. Clifton became the first Chairman and I the Managing Director. He guaranteed the bank overdraft and a small initial salary for myself. He also provided sufficient working capital for the newly formed company to operate.

Clifton Smith-Cox is well-known in the Bristol area. He is a Chartered Accountant and was, at that time, in practice as such. He is one of Bristol's leading and most respected businessmen. Having his name associated with the company was likely to be very helpful to me.

Once the company was formed and marketing took place, the business did expand rapidly. We became well-known for our individual style of products and quality of workmanship.

Clifton and I continued in association together for very many years until after the fire, about which you will read later in this book. He remained Chairman during the rebuilding of the business and the acquisition of new premises, by which time the size had grown into something far more than just a small family business.

It was agreed that outside interests should become involved, and after one unsuitable experience in this con-nection, John (Jack) Sloan Wilson, a former executive of Letraset Limited provided the outside backing necessary. Some years later Jack married my daughter, Alison, and they are now jointly running the factory.

Although Clifton ceased to be Chairman at this time, our friendship has continued to this day, and so has his interest in Peggy Nisbet Limited.

Clifton Smith-Cox, Chairman, Peggy Nisbet Limited.

CHAPTER V

Our First Work-room
─────1950s─────

Now that we had our small work-room, we were able to increase our production.

Most of my readers will know of Norah Wellings. Norah had for many years made *Sailor* dolls for the Cunard Line and many other of the passenger ships. After she retired, the Cunard company approached me and asked if I would make similar *Sailor* dolls. I knew Norah Wellings, so I asked her if we could come to some arrangement by which she would allow me to make her little *Sailors*, which she had designed and which had become world famous.

She told me that she had no objection at all to my making the *Sailors* and wished me luck. She also asked me if I would excuse her if she did not supply me with any patterns because she felt she would be giving away something of herself. Norah and her brother had run the factory and I imagine that when she closed it down, she wanted her work to cease also. She wished me every success and would not accept any payment or royalty from me. This popular *Sailor* doll had a jersey cloth bonded to a damp buckram face.

In charge of our new little work-room was Jean Hancock, of whom I have written elsewhere. We decided to buy a cutting machine now that we had the space in which to install it. The *Sailors* had so many little parts that it was almost impossible to cut by hand in any quantity, and this had become a bread and butter line with a guaranteed weekly order from Cunard of one gross (144) dolls per week. By offering a 3¾% cash discount we could then be assured of a weekly cheque, which greatly helped our cash flow. We also supplied the other shipping lines, but the Cunard weekly order was given priority.

Jean was an excellent organizer. A set of parts consisted of 16 pieces cut by knife and strips for the bib which were ripped by hand.

We installed sewing machines and engaged machinists. Every Monday we cut 144 sets of parts. On Tuesday 144 sets were machined and issued to outworkers for stuffing. For this purpose we used kapok. On Wednesday outworkers stuffed the parts and on Thursday the stuffed arms, legs and bodies

Peggy Nisbet *Sailor.*

were machined together, so that by Thursday evening there were 144 completed dolls. On Friday the staff got together. They brushed, checked, sewed the name tags for the appropriate ships on the hats and packed them all ready for despatch.

We did not use these premises for any of our historical and traditional costume dolls, because whilst we could to a certain extent produce the *Sailors* on a belt-line system, there was so much handwork and specialisation in connection with the former, that I did not think we could combine the two types of work with the same staff and with the same manufacturing procedure. It was essential to reserve the most painstaking and dedicated needlewomen for our character dolls, and not waste their talents on work which could be done by less skilled needlewomen. Jean was originally in charge of the production of our souvenir range of *Happy* dolls marketed under the name of "Tower Treasures" but now that she was responsible for the *Sailors*, the production of the 6in (15cm) *Happy* doll range was integrated with the 7in (18cm) historical range.

New outworkers started with the *Happy* dolls and as they became more expert, they were put on to the more detailed and intricate 7in (18cm) dolls.

The rooms in the flat were soon turned into offices. We now needed someone to do the packing, keep the stock of boxed dolls and despatch the orders. We needed a bookkeeper to write up the books and do the banking, plus a typist to deal with correspondence and invoices.

Malcolm Bowman and Sylvia Bird were engaged within a few weeks of each other. I have referred to them both elsewhere in this book. The banking and ledgers were dealt with by a retired bank manager who came in parttime, and we also had a cheerful little typist/telephonist.

We must now be talking about the early sixties, because my husband died in 1959, and it was at that time that we moved the business out of the house, albeit still into the temporary accommodation described above. We continued in this way until we acquired our first factory.

Jean Hancock.

Our First Trade Fair, U.K.

1957

In 1956 we became members of the B.T.M.A. (The British Toy Manufacturers' Association) and took what was to us a very big step. We decided to take space at the 3rd British Toy Fair, organised by the B.T.M.A., which was to take place at Brighton in January 1957.

Brigadier Drummond, well-known in local amateur dramatic circles, built a superb display unit which was an exact replica of a full-size stage set made to scale for our dolls. It was designed to look like Hampton Court, the palace built by King Henry VIII for Queen Anne Boleyn. It had a wide terrace, with steps to the right and left wings, descending to a lower garden level. The photograph shows our very first display of dolls before we introduced our range of high impact polystyrene figures.

Neither Bill nor I had ever attended a trade fair so we had no idea what was in store for us. The company did not possess a van at that time so we decided to take our samples and scenery by train. In order to get to Brighton from Weston, we had to go via London, where we had not only a change of trains, but a change of stations, from Paddington to Victoria, which entailed going from one side of the city to the other. The scenery and samples travelled in the luggage van of the train. When we arrived at Paddington, we could not find a taxi driver who would take the scenery to Victoria Station. Finally, we found one who was prepared to carry our props, but when we loaded them onto his vehicle, we could not close the door because the scenery, even when not assembled, was too long. Fortunately for us, the driver was a humourous, good-tempered fellow, so he told Bill to sit on the back seat and hang onto the door, which had to be left slightly open, although this was strictly against the regulations. I followed in another taxi with the cartons of samples. From Victoria Station to Brighton everything went into the luggage van.

At this time there was no main exhibition centre in Brighton, so the exhibitors were each allocated a room in a hotel in which to mount their display. To our horror we found that apart from the large manufacturers, who were given the ballroom and other reception rooms, all the smaller exhibitors, including ourselves, had been given bedrooms in which to mount their exhibits. We could not believe our eyes when we were shown into the room.

Admittedly, all the furniture had been removed, but how were we going to disguise a wash-basin? We had taken lengths of velvet and a roll of grey cotton cloth with us in case it might be required, so we draped the latter over the offending basin and erected some shelves in front of it. We ran out of drawing pins, nails and tape, but there was a great camaraderie amongst all the exhibitors, and we all popped in and out of each other's rooms, borrowing and lending one thing or another. We drew the curtains over the window and centered

the miniature stage scenery in front. This now completed one side of the room. We erected grey cloth-covered shelves along two other sides of the room. The bottom shelf had a valance reaching to the ground and behind this we put boxes, cartons, surplus price lists and anything else we wanted to hide.

It was 3 a.m. before we finished.

We had reserved a bedroom in the same hotel, which was on another floor, so we just fell into bed for three hours and asked for a call at 6 a.m. so that we could put the finishing touches to our display.

After breakfast in our room, we went straight to our showroom. It had been swept and cleaned, and we had set out our display the night before, so after adjusting one or two things we sat down to wait for customers.

What agonies we went through for the first two hours. No one had told me that apart from some of the older established exhibitors who had made previous appointments with their customers, the majority of buyers started by visiting stands on the ground floor and worked their way upwards. We were on the third floor! By mid-morning no buyer had appeared and I had become convinced that no one would ever visit us or see our display, and that we would have worked ourselves to a standstill, and incurred all that expense, to no avail.

Suddenly buyers started to arrive. Some placed small sample orders; others took price lists, made notes and said they would come back later in the fair. I did not place much reliance on these promises to return and thought they were merely being polite, still unaware that when contemplating stocking a new line, buyers frequently went through the literature and if interested, decided to come back before the end of the fair or, alternatively, send in their orders subsequently by mail. My naivete and inexperience were monumental.

Bill and I had ordered sandwiches and coffee to be brought to our room at 1 p.m., but I suggested that before then he might like to go down to the cocktail bar and have a beer whilst I held the fort. He had only been gone about a quarter of an hour when he erupted from the lift, which was just outside our room, and rushed over to me where I was somewhat disconsolately re-arranging the display. Now my husband was a very quiet, slow moving, undemonstrative and calm Scotsman, who rarely showed any kind of emotion, but his face was wreathed in smiles. He said, "What do you think? I have just been standing in the lounge alongside one of the biggest U.K. buyers who was talking to one of his colleagues. He said, 'You must go up to the Peggy Nisbet stand on the third floor. They have a range of historical costume dolls different from any I have ever seen. I have never heard of them before, but I am going back to place an order so that I can make a full display in the store.' "

Hampton Court Display at Brighton Toy Fair, 1957.

For the remainder of the fair we had a steady stream of buyers.

News of the dolls spread by word of mouth, and we took sufficient orders to justify the cost of the toy fair, in addition to which we received repeat orders throughout the remainder of the year. We still supply many of those, our oldest customers, who opened accounts with us on that day.

We received assistance from the B.T.M.A. officials and from our fellow exhibitors. The Allen family was particularly helpful. They are the creators of the popular "Fuzzyfelt" games, which many of my readers will have bought for their children. Lois Allen still designs her delightful little characters, animals and flowers. Her son, Richard, has replaced his father, who died a few years ago, as managing director. Richard is the very active vice-chairman of the B.T.H.A. (British Toys and Hobbies Association). Every year at Brighton our two families had a celebration dinner at the same restaurant and at the same table. One year at the New York Toy Fair we had the additional help of Lois's sister, Evelyn Crawford, and step-daughter, Diana Hearne, who with her lawyer husband, Bob, frequently offered me the hospitality of their home. My son, Peter, and his wife, Mary, represented our company at one of the early New York Toy Fairs and first made the acquaintance of the Allens who have since become such firm friends. We all still visit each other regularly, both in England and the U.S.A.

I have very happy memories of the Brighton Toy Fairs now, alas, held in London. The staff at The Grand and Metropole Hotels, at which we exhibited and stayed, received and welcomed us year after year. As a matter of interest, the rooms occupied by Margaret Thatcher and her cabinet when a bomb exploded, killing and severely injuring leading members of the Conservative Party in 1984, were the very ones that we had stayed in ourselves.

The B.B.C. occupied a suite on the same floor during the fairs where they gave some memorable parties hosted by Roy Williams of B.B.C. Television Enterprises. In the sixties we were producing many of the characters in the B.B.C. children's programmes including Parsley, Dill and Sage of "The Herbs" programme and also Mr. & Mrs. Pogle, Tog and Pippin of "The Pogles" series. They were wonderful parties which continued into the early hours of the morning, with guests sitting around on the floor. There was much hilarious chatting and badinage as we all unwound after the day's hard work. For fairs are tiring. It is not only the standing and the heat and the dry atmosphere. One is selling one's creations; listening to suggestions; watching for reactions. Adrenalin runs high, but afterwards one feels drained of energy. However, one revives by the next morning, and the excitement starts all over again. For it is exciting, and my enthusiasm never waned.

During the fair there were meetings, cocktail parties, receptions and banquets when all the members of the toy industry got together to discuss new trends and business generally. These functions are an important part of the fairs, when so much business is discussed and decisions made.

On the last night of the fair, we used to make up a large dinner party at Wheeler's famous Fish Restaurant with friends, new and old.

On the occasion of our first toy fair, which I have just described, we were still "new boys" and only knew the people we had just met, so Bill and I had a quiet dinner and went to bed early.

The next morning was bright and sunny, although it was still January with a bitterly cold wind blowing. Bill and I walked along the seafront to the town centre, and we celebrated by Bill taking me into the leading store to buy a hat. I have always loved hats and I can well remember the model I bought there. It is still packed away somewhere in my attic.

Then it was back to the factory to put in production the orders we had taken, and to share with the staff the success we had achieved. Their enthusiasm and pleasure in our success was as great as mine, and they all worked like Trojans to get the orders despatched.

We have never had one disappointing fair in all the years we have exhibited. I always found them exhilarating and tremendously enjoyable, despite all the hard work involved. It was a wonderful experience to be able to talk to our buyers with our whole range on view, and to discuss the merits and demerits of various characters and costumes. One learnt so much, and this personal contact with our customers was of inestimable value. I would take voluminous notes of their comments. Always to hand was a thick pad of yellow memorandum paper and a page was devoted to each customer. On my return to the office I would go through my notes to see if there was any way in which we could improve our range. I never disregarded any constructive criticism or suggestion, both being always welcome.

In 1974 we experienced what is now referred to as "The three-day week." At one point factories were only able to use electricity for three days a week. This period coincided with the time that we were preparing samples for trade fairs, so the main part of our machining had to be done on those three days.

For the rest of the week Mabel Perry used my personal and treasured old Singer treadle machine. Sadly a member of the staff must have decided to trade it in without my authorization when he bought new electric industrial machines and I never saw it again. It was of great sentimental value because Auntie Kitty had made some of our earliest samples with it. During the strike we bought oil heaters for warmth and small oil stoves for heating food and hot drinks.

Despite these setbacks, our samples were ready for the fairs, and I sincerely believe that the staff enjoyed meeting the challenge, despite the temporary inconvenience.

In the years to come, we participated in many other fairs, in addition to toy fairs, because our dolls were sold through gift shops and speciality shops; in boutiques, on liners, planes, airports and a host of other outlets, but I have always had a very soft spot for the B.T.M.A. whose members were so helpful to us in establishing U.K. and world markets.

The old B.T.M.A. (British Toy Manufacturers Association) referred to previously has now become the B.T.H.A. (British Toy & Hobby Manufacturers Association).

The Director General and Secretary, D.L. Hawtin, FCIS, has replaced Gordon Goude, MBE, who served in that capacity for many years. Most of the leading figures in the toy industry have served on the committee and become chairmen over the years. Even when I was a newcomer and completely unknown, they all treated me with the greatest courtesy.

Arthur Katz, CBE, of Corgi Toys, Denis Britain, OBE, of toy soldiers fame, Roger Swinburne-Johnson of Chad Valley, Leslie Smith, OBE, of Matchbox Toys, Torquil Norman of Bluebird Toys and Tom Cassidy of Cassidy Bros. are a few of the eminent names who have built the British toy industry. The present chairman is Ian Scott of Dean's Rag Book Co. and the Vice-Chairman Richard Allen of Allen Industries (Fuzzy-felt). To all of these, and the others not mentioned, I extend my thanks.

John Glanville was indefatigable in organizing trade fairs. He has now been succeeded by Simon Osborn whilst the popular Tommy Thomas is still engaged in writing about them.

It was an honour to be asked by the B.T.M.A. in latter years to serve on the Wages Council, which I did for many years. It was an interesting and enjoyable experience.

Up with Sales and Down with Drinks!

Brighton Toy Fair —
B.T.M.A. Reception.
Early 1970s.

M. S. Macgregor of Peggy Nisbet, Mr. Allan of Allan Industries Ltd., Mrs. Peggy Nisbet, Mrs. Allan, and Mr. M. J. Bowman of Peggy Nisbet.

Creation of the Peggy Nisbet Standard Doll

1950s

All my efforts at finding a suitable medium for the production of my own doll having proved unavailing, I decided that my next step would have to be the investigation of some kind of injection moulding process. I had been reluctant to try this method for several reasons. First, I did not want the doll to have the shiny appearance of the plastic dolls then available; secondly, it was essential that the doll should not be too light in weight, otherwise the sometimes heavy brocade dresses of the Elizabethan era would not hang properly; thirdly, the cost of the moulds would assuredly be prohibitive; fourthly, large quantities of dolls would have to be moulded at one time in order to make it an economic proposition and I did not want to mass produce. Finally, I knew that the highly tempered steel moulds which would be necessary would have to be made by a skilled engraver working from my original model, so however good he might be, I should only be getting a craftsman's impression of an artist's work, not the original model itself. Above all, I wanted to make dolls of interesting people whose characters would show in their faces and who would be easily recognisable. With tools costing in excess of £1,000 each (which was a considerable sum in the fifties), I had not the finance to do more than a few, nor would it be practical to invest these sums for dolls which were not to be produced in quantity.

I was extremely fortunate in that when making my enquiries I had been introduced to Harry Dunkley, who had worked in plastics since this medium was in its infancy. Harry had been working for a small firm and then formed his own company, Mornings Limited. He became interested in our problem and devised a method of moulding a solid doll. This was, of course, more expensive because of the large quantity of plastic used in the moulding process, but it produced the result I wanted. The usual method of producing dolls was to mould the back and front separately and then stick the two thin halves, or shells of the figure, together, thus making a lightweight flimsy doll. I insisted upon weight, so it had to be solid. There were many difficulties, particularly one known as "sinking" due to the bulk of material in one area. This was evidenced in our *Henry VIII* figure, when his fat tummy would sink during the normal moulding process. Harry overcame this.

Another problem with injection moulding was that when modelling, we had to avoid undercuts so that the doll could be withdrawn easily from the mould. Again *Henry* was a problem because of his characteristic stance.

Nearly all his portraits, particularly as an older man, show

him with his feet planted well apart and turned outwards. There was only one answer to this: the body had to be moulded in one piece down to the ankles, and the feet moulded separately, so that they could be joined at the ankle, spreading outwards. This was done by a hole being bored in the ankle and a fine pin inserted in the leg. Glue was added to ensure strength.

We have had a few complaints over the years that *Henry's* feet have broken at the ankle. This is not the case. In each instance the doll has probably had a sharp knock on the thinnest part of the ankle which has dislodged the foot, breaking it away from the upper part of the leg.

I am glad to be able to explain this to collectors, although it rarely happens because the styrene we use is virtually unbreakable. The feet can easily be put on again with a dab of glue, and the join will be invisible.

Whilst this development was taking place, I had paid innumerable visits to laboratories and factories working in plastic materials in order to find a suitable "mix." I was still determined to find a formula which would produce a matt flesh-like appearance and not the shiny glassy surface associated with existing plastic dolls.

Then there was the colour, as well as the texture, to consider. No one would believe the varying tones of colour offered to me as "flesh." They varied from pale creams right through to dark murky beiges or highly coloured crimsons which looked as though the dolls were suffering from an overdose of sun! Finally, we found a suitable material, with an acceptable colour which we have always tried to maintain. Plastics, and colours in particular, have become more stable and sophisticated in recent years, and the same problems no longer exist.

Concurrently with the research taking place into moulding materials, I still had to deal with the problem of moulds: one being dependent upon the other. As on previous occasions, the result of my many and varied enquiries produced a coming together of skills, and consequent consistency of high quality workmanship in the production of our dolls which has lasted to this day.

It is difficult, nay impossible, to describe all this in chronological order, and in ensuing chapters I shall have to go back to earlier developments.

I cannot remember the exact sequence of events. It was still in the fifties, and I was now liaising with three acknowledged experts in their own fields: Mr. Robson, familiarly known as Robbie, was with The London and

Sculptures by
RONALD CAMERON

An artist with a world wide reputation for realistic figurative work, mainly in silver and bronze. His specific skills are much sought after by sports organisations for prize trophies. He has made sculptures of every conceivable sport from cricket to darts from swimming to gymnastics.

A demand is growing for Ronald Camerons unique sculptures in TERRA COTTA. Each figure is individually modelled and then kiln fired. This method of production guarantees the originality of every piece.

Ronald Cameron.

Ron trained at Camberwell (London) School of Art from 1946 to 1950. He has made trophies for many prestigious awards, including sporting organisations and has worked for television and film companies, as well as producing original models of zoo animals for the toy trade. He is very versatile. This is demonstrated by the following models, the likenesses of which he has caught in each case: *Queen Elizabeth II, Queen Elizabeth the Queen Mother, Prince Philip, Prince Charles, Princess Anne, Pope John Paul, Pope John XIII, Charlie Chaplin, Margaret Thatcher, President Reagan* - a more varied group of characters it would be difficult to find.

Over the years we have evolved a procedure whereby we have mouldings made of a complete male doll and a complete female doll, known in the factory as our standard male and standard female. This is our original Peggy Nisbet doll and is used for all models other than portrait character dolls, which are individually moulded.

In order to make a character doll we use the unique process by which Rotoplas supplies the tools to make perfect reproductions of the original models. It is an electroforming process, which I have asked Robbie to describe in his own words because collectors will surely be interested. By this process one can achieve an exact reproduction of the original model, not an engraver's interpretation of a fellow artist's work.

I must go back a little. Having found an ideal manufacturing process, it was essential that I should devise a way in which I could use it with the limited finances at my disposal. The cost of an electroformed tool being so high, it seemed that I should only be able to buy a very few, and here was I contemplating not only a standard male and standard female doll, but also British monarchs from 1066 A.D. up to the 1980s and members of the present royal family, a period of nearly 1000 years.

With the help of my "Doll Production Team" who liaised with me and with each other, we developed the idea of having a few basic figures to which we could affix a portrait head or a head and shoulders. Our first effort was to cut off the head at the neck, but this idea was very short-lived because we would have an ugly neck join, however skilfully done. We then tried cutting off the top part of the body below the bust line. This would enable us to have each character modelled complete with its neck and shoulders, which would be of different dimensions.

Scandinavian Metallurgical Co. Limited. He is now Managing Director of Rotoplas Limited. His Co-Director is Dave Ellis, a talented engineer, whom I had not met at that time. Harry Dunkley (plastics) and Robbie (Rotoplas), later joined by Dave Ellis (Rotoplas) and Ronald Cameron (sculptor), formed a team which has produced our dolls over three decades.

Ronald Cameron is a sculptor who has made many of our character dolls and has, therefore, worked closely with Rotoplas and Mornings.

A word from Rotoplas Limited -
Toolmakers to the Plastics Industry

"It was in the 1950's that we had the pleasure of being consulted by Peggy Nisbet with regard to producing tooling for the manufacture of the various body parts for the dressed dolls that have become internationally famous.

"It was emphasised that it was essential to reproduce to perfection the detail of the models to be supplied, thus not losing any of the creative skills of the sculptor.

"To achieve this by conventional toolmaking would have been virtually impossible but as we were engaged in the use of a process known as Electroforming, we were able to comply with this requirement, down to the finest scratch.

"For the technically interested Electroforming is a highly developed form of electroplating but in this case heavy deposits of Nickel or sometimes Copper are built up on to a non conductive material to a determined thickness sufficient to allow external machining of the resultant electroform - as it is called - to a suitable geometrical shape for use in an injection mould...

"...To enable plating to take place the models are coated with a film of silver, infinitesimal in thickness.

"The usual procedure in providing patterns suitable for plating is that the sculptor firstly creates the form in modelling clay. From this, plaster casts are made, in segment form if necessary, to permit removal of the pattern. These casts are then used to produce epoxy resin patterns which are ideal for plating...

"...We are very pleased to have been associated with the project and have enjoyed the friendly relationship with Peggy Nisbet and her colleagues during the intervening years and which still exists."

Ron Barbier.

Close-up of *Queen Elizabeth II.*

At this point I should explain that whilst the tool for a complete doll using the electroforming process was expensive, we could obtain small head and shoulder moulds at a comparatively low price; moreover, we could purchase a small moulding machine which we could use in our own factory and thus mould in small quantities. These, however, will only take a small quantity of plastic for each head, so there had to be a very close working relationship between the modeller, the toolmaker and myself. Rotoplas has made some beautiful tools for us over the years, and they are just as good to-day as they were 30 years ago.

Finally, we decided to go ahead with tools for our original standard male and female Peggy Nisbet dolls and *Henry VIII.* At a later date we added two tools: the standard male torso only (from the feet to the neck) and the standard female (from the feet to just below the bust).

We now mould all our portrait heads in our own factory, and are thus able to meet collectors' requests for new models every year to add to their collections.

There have been two exceptions to our normal procedure of fixing a portrait head onto a body of the same material. A few years ago I had an overwhelming desire to produce dolls of Tutankhamun and Nefertiti. I borrowed books from the library, made numerous visits to the Egyptology Section of the British Museum, and for a while lived and dreamed Egypt and the Egyptians.

For a long time I could not imagine how I was going to make the doll itself, with its unique features and spectacular headdress. Then, suddenly, I had an inspiration and the very

next day, in a great state of enthusiasm and excitement, I sped up the motorway to visit Ronald Barbier.

Ron Barbier is another of Britain's leading craftsmen, whom I first commissioned to make the master pattern for The Imperial State Crown. Dembo, the Bristol jewellers, had made a silver model previously, which was just ready for the pattern maker, when it was destroyed in our factory fire where I had locked it up in my office. A photograph which I had taken of the original Dembo crown is shown in this book and, of course, Ron Barbier's crown appears on all the latter models of *Queen Elizabeth II* in her State Robes.

I asked Ron Barbier to tell me about some of his commissions and quote from his reply:

"...Having completed nearly 50 years in the making of Gold, Silver and Bronze works, I can now look back with great satisfaction at the pleasure and pride it has given me and hopefully my customers, both trade and private; commissions carried out to their exact requirements, at the same time allowing myself a bit of artist's licence to work to practical requirements.

"Over the years my work has covered Church work in all metals, and quite a wide range of Civic Regalia...

"My first work with Mrs. Nisbet involved making a master pattern for the Imperial State Crown.

"Still with Royalty, models were made of The Queen Mother's Tiara, Necklace and her various Orders of Merit. Then came models for The Prince

Imperial State Crown and Sceptre.

of Wales Insignia and Orders of Merit.

"A pattern for The Pope's Staff was also an addition to the Nisbet range of dolls.

"A model of the Peggy Nisbet motif was also made..."

The model of the Peggy Nisbet motif to which Ron Barbier refers will be remembered by the many hundreds of collectors to whom I have presented them during my overseas tours, and on many other occasions. It was designed by Sue Worth.

After a most interesting discussion Ron and I decided that for *Tutankhamun* we would use a different technique. He made a master pattern of the Pharaoh's face and headdress, then had it moulded in metal. This was painted and slipped over the head and shoulders of our standard male doll, the body of which had been painted a tan colour to represent an Egyptian. It is a magnificent piece of work. When we introduced our *Nefertiti* model the following year, we used the same procedure.

No doubt others could have developed a doll with much less exertion, and in a shorter time, but I knew nothing about plastics, nothing about tooling or moulds (other than for china) so it was trial and error all the way. It was only with the enthusiastic assistance of such a skilled group of craftsmen that I was able to achieve any result. I am glad to have this opportunity of paying tribute to them and the contribution they made to the Peggy Nisbet Story.

An early model of *Anne Boleyn.*

38

Our First Factory

———1960s———

Malcolm Bowman holding *Henry VIII*.

Our first factory was an old two-storey building which had previously been used as a furniture warehouse. It was situated at 59A Whitecross Road, and was only a few hundred yards away from the seafront. There was plenty of space but there was the problem of carrying materials, dolls and boxes from one floor to another.

By this time we had a telephonist, who also did errands and saw to the post. We had an invoice clerk and a bookkeeper. In charge of these three was Sylvia Bird. I had my own secretary, Mary Maloney, who was an excellent shorthand typist; she was very quiet but with a great sense of humour. My son-in-law, Michael Fox, was in charge of the factory and on the sales side was Malcolm Bowman. Upstairs in our workrooms we had cutters, machinists, finishers, girls in charge of materials, dolls and accessories and artists to paint the dolls. In charge of the workroom itself was Jean Hancock, promoted from her first little workroom, who was like a

human dynamo: never still for a moment, with her eyes never missing a thing.

The discipline upon which I insisted in the factory was, I suppose, strict by to-day's standards but the atmosphere was always cheerful and apart from an occasional argument or complaint, there was the usual hum of activity produced by the clatter of the sewing machines and the chatter of the machinists. There was only one serious disharmony, over a decade later, and that was during the brief period when the Design Department was based at The Tower. The factory manager had to submit weekly production figures to the Board, but if he did not achieve his target he would report that it was because the Design Department had not sent him the prototypes and patterns. The truth was that frequently he had omitted to order some of the materials required so the samples could not be made but he would never admit to his negligence. The design staff, who worked hard to keep to their schedule were frustrated and bitterly resented the unjust accusation of holding up production. Other than this, the staff were extraordinarily loyal to each other throughout the whole of my doll-making years.

When engaging staff I would look for enthusiasm, willingness, a pleasant personality and above all, common sense, rather than academic qualifications, and this was undoubtedly the reason why we had such excellent and long-serving employees.

We have always employed a group of skilled needlewomen to whom we refer as "outworkers" in addition to our factory staff. When we first moved into the Whitecross Road factory, most of them brought in their work weekly. This was checked at a counter near the entrance to the factory, after which they were paid and issued with the next week's work. Any problems which they encountered were ironed out on the spot.

As the volume of our orders increased, we had to employ more and more outworkers, until eventually we decided to buy a van and deliver the work to them instead of using their time to come to the factory. Most of them lived locally, and all of them within a radius of 20 miles. We made two rounds a week. Eventually we required two vans, making rounds every day of the week, sometimes doing two or three trips daily. This required a full-time driver who could also check the work.

In the early days, before we could afford a full-time driver, my daughter-in-law, Mary, took the work to our outworkers, and later on my daughter, Alison, took over the job.

Alison had a baby, James, and was pregnant with her second child, Felicity. She put James in the back of the car in a Karrycot amongst the skips of work for outworkers. The

Henry VIII and Wives, 1960s - first factory.

largest round was in Bristol which is 20 miles from Weston and James had to be fed and his nappy changed.

You will have read earlier in this book about our first group of outworkers in Bristol. By lunch time Alison reached Gerda Slade, who is very cheerful and hospitable. Alison went into her house, where James had his bottle and was changed, whilst Gerda, who is an excellent cook, produced a home-made cake and a pot of tea. Thus refreshed, Alison was able to go on her way.

After Felicity was born, Alison took the two babies with her, and Auntie Kitty sat in the car so that Alison could drive without being distracted by the children.

Now that the factory was organised, and production going comparatively smoothly, we needed to enlarge our order book. There had never been any necessity to advertise because there were always sufficient orders coming in to match our making capacity but if we wanted to expand, we should have to widen our market.

I have never spent much money on advertising in glossy magazines or on television. We were fortunate in that we always had plenty of free publicity. Articles, photographs of our dolls and editorials appeared regularly, with no cost to ourselves. When we introduced topical characters, the tele-vision studios would contact us, either to visit our factory and film the manufacturing processes, or else they would invite me to the studios to be interviewed and show our dolls. This happened not only locally but also on the national network in the United Kingdom and in nearly every city I visited in the U.S.A.

My advertising budget was, therefore, used almost entirely on participating in trade fairs and exhibitions, both here and abroad. Many of these were subsidized by the Board of Trade, now the Department of Trade and Industry.

As the business grew, I had to spend more and more time in administration and organisation. One of my faults is that I am not good at delegating responsibility. Perfection is my goal so it is impossible for me to resist checking up to make sure that my instructions are being carried out correctly. I could never see the point of delegating jobs to such an extent that one was out of touch with problems, even small ones. So much can go wrong so quickly and it is surprising how few people have good judgement and foresight and, therefore, cannot appreciate the difference between a minor and major problem, tackling it only when it is too late to solve it. I was determined to avoid this situation. The only way in which I could do this was to keep myself informed by day to day personal contact with each department. The business was small enough to be able to do this. Had my staff been larger, I would have been obliged to delegate and would have had to distribute grandiose titles such as "Head of Department," "Departmental Manager," "Administrator," and so forth, which would, in fact, only be status symbols. This I deplore. It would have resulted in "all Chiefs and no Indians," plus innumerable staff meetings. My dedicated little staff would have ceased to work as a team, and the whole success of our happy little work-room was based on team-work, enthusiasm and loyalty. Visitors to the factory invariably remarked on the cheerful and friendly atmosphere, yet I was not able to pay very high salaries nor did the factory have any luxuries: only basic facilities.

Amongst members of the staff there are three, all of them still with us, who were the real builders of the business and without whom the company would never have flourished. Malcolm Bowman, Mabel Perry and Sylvia Bird have been with me for over 25 years. They have stood by me loyally, through good times and bad for, as in all businesses, we have had our ups and downs. All three would turn their hands to anything in an emergency without moaning or groaning, leaving their own specific jobs to help wherever required and working late if need be.

Malcolm Bowman joined us in 1961. He had been a salesman in Cornwall, then went to America with his wife, Jean, and their young family. They decided to return to England and he applied to me for a job because he was living in a lovely old farmhouse, only ten miles from Weston, which had been in Jean's family for very many years. He was first employed to take charge of despatches and produce stock control records which he submitted to me weekly. However, over the years he has at one time or another worked in every department and is now Sales Director of The House of Nisbet Ltd. There is nothing about the business that he does not know, but his real love is making sales trips and attending fairs. He has built up a close relationship with many of our customers, by whom he is well liked.

He has been deeply involved in the business and taken pride in its growth. On many occasions he has worked day and night, not only erecting our display stands, but also designing and making them.

When we employed new staff, it was Malcolm who instructed them in moulding procedures, painting, machining, cutting - you name it, he knows it. After my husband died in 1959, Malcolm accompanied me on our annual Scottish and other sales trips.

Malcolm has a wife, Jean, two sons and one daughter living in Australia. They are all married.

Sylvia Bird joined us at almost the same time as Malcolm. She started with us as bookkeeper, then as our clerical staff grew, she was put in sole charge of accounts and banking, responsible directly to me and the chairman for supplying a monthly trial balance sheet. When our cash flow was difficult, as it was frequently, Sylvia would spend half an hour with me every morning going through our lists of debtors and creditors to see how we could get in money owing to us in order to pay our own bills.

Sylvia is discretion itself, and not once in all these years has she ever betrayed a confidence or leaked any information regarding staff salaries and wages or company finances. She has always worked well with Malcolm Bowman and Mabel Perry. When Alison and I were in the U.S.A. on trade missions or fairs, we left the three in charge of the factory, knowing that in any emergency they would together deal with it and only contact us if any difficulty arose with which they could not cope.

Another way in which Sylvia was helpful was at trade fairs. Although strictly not part of her duties, each year she accompanied us to the toy fairs and gift fairs; she assisted in the siting of the display units and the disposition of the dolls; she attended to customers throughout the fair, and finally she made herself responsible for what to the layman might appear to be unimportant but which to us was invaluable. Being a very practical person, she personally assembled and packed pens, pads, order forms, price lists, catalogues and all the paraphernalia required at fairs. She also wrote up the expense sheets (I could never remember to get receipts at restaurants, or keep a record of tips to workmen and other disbursements.) but Sylvia followed me round and jotted them all down, which greatly pleased our accountants.

There is one episode which neither Sylvia nor I will ever forget. It took place at the Brighton Toy Fair in 1970. We had worked into the early hours of the morning. After a few hours sleep and an early breakfast, we went to our stand about 20 minutes before the fair opened. She had left it all ready the night before, so only had to take down the cover sheets and check up that everything was in order. When we arrived on the stand we saw a handwritten note. It was an order for 8000 each of the three Dick Bruna characters for which we had only just obtained the licence and which we had produced as soft toys, using a design by one of our staff, Pam Crook; Creative Playthings had bought 24,000 of our new soft toy which we were producing by the silkscreen process for distribution in the U.S.A. We could not believe our eyes. The buyer had, presumably, been allowed into the fair in order to have a preview of the exhibits because he had to fly to the Nurnberg Fair that morning, as it ran concurrently with the Brighton Toy Fair, so he left the order on the stand.

This was followed by another exciting episode. We sold out our Limited Edition the first day. It was one of our most successful fairs.

Finally, but by no means least, there is Mabel Perry. Mabel Perry is an attractive widow in her sixties, and she has worked with me for 23 years. She is an exquisite needlewoman with an infinite amount of patience, and she is completely wrapped up in the dolls: each character she helps to create becomes a living person. I do not know what I should do without her.

Mabel has a son, John, who is an executive with British Petroleum. John has had several posts in the Middle East where he lives with his wife, Ann, and daughter, Amy. His son is a student at Cheltenham College. Mabel's daughter, another Anne, lives with her husband and three sons in Birmingham.

In May 1959 my husband went to the hospital for a check-up and the doctors diagnosed lung cancer. He had always been so healthy and we were devastated. It was too far advanced to operate, so I took him by ambulance to our little Scottish house in Leitholm, Scotland, in the village he loved. I left Alison and Brigitte in charge of the factory and every alternate week I caught the sleeper leaving Berwick-on-Tweed at 8 p.m., travelling via London and arriving at Weston at 11 a.m. the next morning. After a meeting lasting all the afternoon, I caught the night train back to Berwick-on-Tweed, arriving back in Scotland at breakfast time. By travelling overnight both ways, I was only away from Leitholm for one day so Bill did not have time to miss me. I took ledgers back with me and was able to work on them and keep them up to date.

The doctors had given Bill two months to live, but he survived long enough to celebrate our Silver Wedding Anniversary in June. He died on 6th October. He would have loved to see the growth of the company but it was not to be.

Alison was still at school when I first started making dolls, but inevitably she got sucked into the maelstrom of the family business and became familiar with all its aspects.

My mother helped me by going to the local shops and bringing back short trial lengths of cloth, ribbons and lace with which to make prototypes. She brought books from the library, and did all my shopping for me which was a great help.

After Bill died, Alison became indispensable to me. Her great love is music, and at one time she contemplated training to be a concert pianist, but she decided to help me run the company, and I can never thank her enough for the hard work and support she has given me over the years.

However, she has not neglected her musical talents. Her love of the piano has been superseded by her love of the organ, and as I write this book, she is Director of Music at the Church of St. John The Baptist of Weston-super-Mare, in addition to acting as Design Director and assisting her husband, Jack Wilson, to run the company. Jack is now Chairman and Managing Director of The House of Nisbet. He married Alison on 9th June 1976, the anniversary of my own wedding day.

Alison has three children by her first marriage, to Michael Fox: James, aged 24, who joined a Bristol firm of stockbrokers after leaving Cambridge University two years ago. Felicity, aged 23, who is at Edinburgh University, and Charlotte, aged 21, who is taking an advanced business course after having completed a secretarial course at Oxford. Jack and Alison have two young children, William, aged 9 who is at Tewkesbury Abbey Choir School and Clementine, aged 4, who is still at playschool.

It is impossible to list all my staff - there have been too many over the years, but mention must be made of Sylvia Hooper, who was our first artist and started painting dolls' faces in the early fifties. When we moved into the factory she was put in charge of the art-room. She is still painting for us.

Brigitte Charsley was with us in the early days, but left when her two daughters, Colette and Claire, were born. Now that her children have left home, she is back at the factory assisting Alison in the Design Department.

Michael Fox was General Manager in the sixties succeeded by Michael McGregor, a young man with an engaging personality who had worked in the City of London as a stockbroker and moved to Weston with his family.

Mrs. McClements, known as Mrs. Mac, was a work-room manageress for some years.

Dorothy Mantle has contributed much to the company, but she did not join us until after the fire, when we were installed in our first Oldmixon factory. My first secretary, Mary Maloney, had left us and I interviewed several applicants with a view to replacing her. Having decided to employ one girl, I interviewed Dorothy later the same day. She was a first class shorthand typist and appeared to be particularly intelligent and competent, so I engaged her as well. Alison was now working with me as Joint Managing Director. We both had more work than we could cope with and each of us needed an assistant to take over some of our tasks so it was an admirable arrangement. Dorothy is now in overall charge of the office staff, the computer and accounts of The House of Nisbet Ltd.

A member of the staff who has been with us for many years, and who must have boxed many thousands of dolls, is Marie Wills. When Marie joined us as a school leaver, she was deaf and dumb. Her family wanted to put her into a Council home, but we offered her a job. She was unable to get to work on her own, but Jean Hancock met her off the bus each morning, and put her on again in the evening. Throughout the years Jean encouraged her to form words and lip-read until Marie could communicate with her colleagues. It was entirely due to Jean's interest and patience that Marie became a normal member of society.

Marie Wills and Peggy Nisbet in the Boxing Department at Oldmixon factory, June 1979.

Scotland

—1950s-1984—

Scotland has had a great part to play in the history of our company, both as a market place and as an area in which to manufacture.

My husband, William Wood Nisbet, was a Scot from Edinburgh. He had strong family ties with the Scottish borders, having spent most of his childhood holidays with his grandparents at their home, a cottage in the village of Leitholm, Berwickshire. It was from this little village house which had been in my husband's family since 1776, that we decided to run a cottage industry where we could make all our Scottish models.

Leitholm is near Coldstream, where the famous Regiment of the Coldstream Guards was formed in the 17th century and where the River Tweed divides England from Scotland. Nearby is the old cobblestone town of Kelso where the Duke of Roxburgh owns one of Britain's stately homes called Floors Castle, which has 365 windows, one for each day of the year!

This is the heart of the Sir Walter Scott country to which visitors from all over the world come to tour the beautiful countryside with its lochs and heather-covered hills.

When my husband and I made our first Scottish sales trips, we discovered that the buyers were very anxious that the items they bought were genuinely made in Scotland. This inspired us to use our cottage as a Scottish work-room.

The work was supervised by Isa Purves, the wife of our neighbour, Eddie Purves. Each week Eddie and Isa took the work to needlewomen in their outlying homes on the moors, and collected it the following week, when it was parcelled up and despatched to our main factory in Weston-super-Mare.

Many of the needlewomen led lonely lives, particularly when they were snowed in during the winter, so they enjoyed the intricate and interesting work. They were all very clever with their fingers, and some of the best models we ever produced were made by this little team of skilled needle-

Leitholm, Scotland.

Eddie and Isa Purves.

women. Their handstitching was beautiful, and their love of the work showed in the finished dolls.

In those early days, before my dolls were so well-known abroad, about one third of all the ones we produced were sold in Scotland — and now we were able to print labels which stated that the Scottish models were genuinely made in Scotland.

Our sales increased.

The owner of The Tartan Gift Shop in Edinburgh travelled to Leitholm so that he could call and make sure that the dolls were actually made there, and that we were not just using an accommodation address. They subsequently became one of our biggest customers and often laughed at the way in which they checked up on us.

In 1973 the town council of Coldstream approached me and asked if my company would be interested in buying a small "nursery" factory in a group of units which they were proposing to build to provide employment in the borough and in the surrounding countryside. We were delighted to be asked and negotiations were started.

It was tremendously exciting to inspect the site, see the plans and then to watch the factories being built. I took a few snaps of the buildings in various stages of construction which are reproduced in this book. When the factories were finished, the local council landscaped the area in front of the factory which sloped down to the roadway. The one-storey building with its wooden facia and large full-length picture windows overlooking the Chevoit Hills, which separate Scotland from England, produced a very pleasing effect.

Although small, the interior of the factory was practical. The service doors, wash-rooms and packing department were at the back and the two large work-rooms with their lovely views over the River Tweed and the distant Chevoit Hills, in the front.

Isa Purves, who had previously organized the outworkers from my Leitholm house, now supervised the factory with its small staff. Sadly, both Eddie and Isa died recently.

Dr. Brian Sproule, the local doctor, who was also vice chairman of the council, was largely responsible for the factory project, because he was anxious to create jobs in Coldstream. His wife, Irene, was of great assistance to me.

Since most of my time was spent in the Weston factory, which was 400 miles away, I needed someone upon whom I could rely because I was only able to pay occasional visits to Scotland, but Irene kept me in touch with the staff and their work, and generally deputised for me, despite the fact that as a doctor's wife, she had many responsibilities and great involvement in the social life of the local community.

My lawyer, Mr. Andrew Anderson, senior partner of Melrose & Porteous, solicitors of Coldstream, was also actively involved in the project and his wife, Margaret, has helped me with research. Both the Sproule and Anderson families have become old friends over the years. I am deeply indebted to them for all their help and encouragement, and would like to take this opportunity of paying tribute to their many kindnesses.

Brian and Irene Sproule breed the beautiful and aristocratic looking Pharaoh Hounds which they show at Crufts and other dog shows with great success.

In 1973 the town celebrated the tercentenary of the raising of the Coldstream Guards, and we were asked to make some special models for inclusion in an exhibition which was held in the Town Hall during the Coldstream Week. This is an annual event during which the town presents itself and all its history, not only to Berwickshire and the border country, but to visitors from far and wide. During this celebration all the pageantry and customs of this ancient Scottish borough were displayed in all their glory. Photographs of the models we made appear in this book. They are of particular interest because only one of each was ever made.

Much research went into the design of all our Scottish models. Tartans in miniature "setts" were made for us of 100% wool in Scottish mills. Peatgatherers' baskets and fishermen's creels were made to scale by men in the small fishing villages on the west coast of Scotland during the winter months when they were unable to get out in their boats. Tweeds in Shetland wool were woven for us in small patterns, and hand-knitted shawls were knitted for Peatgatherers and Fisherwomen, and other characters.

I take particular pride in the kilts which we make. Every needlewoman who makes a kilt is trained carefully. Even though in miniature, they are accurate in every detail. Our tartans are all authentic and woven in miniature. The cloth at

Margaret and Andrew Anderson.

Dr. Brian and Irene Sproule.

Scottish group.

Emily Wagstaff (cooking) and Peggy Nisbet at barbecue lunch, Yetholm, Scotland, October 1985.

the Lochcarron Mills in Galashiels is cut to the required length and width; then it is hemmed by machine. This is the only part of the kilt that is not entirely done by hand. After the hem is machined, the cloth is pleated and each pleat pinned into place before being pressed by a warm iron. The pins are then taken out and the bottom of the pleats tacked into place. The tacking is kept there until the finished doll is actually boxed, making sure the pleats are kept in place.

It was impossible to keep stock of all the hundreds of different tartans, so we restricted our models to the well-known and popular Royal Stewart, Dress Stewart, Campbell, Anderson, MacGregor, Macbeth and Cameron. After the fire, as the cost of transporting work and material to and from our two factories increased, and there was less time at my disposal for travelling backwards and forwards between Scotland and England, we finally decided to close the little factory in Coldstream, although our staff continued to sew for us in their own homes as outworkers as they had done in the past. The work was again controlled from my Leitholm cottage, and we also installed there a small moulding machine upon which Eddie Purves moulded heads and small accessories such as guns, garter stars, sporran tops and bagpipes. The pouch of the sporrans was made from genuine sealskin, which we bought as offcuts from one of the leading manufacturers of sporrans. For those of you not familiar with Scottish Highland Dress, the sporran is a large pouch or purse usually made of sealskin, worn hanging from the belt in front of the kilt.

It was a great sorrow to me when we decided to close our Scottish factory. I had watched it being built and although we had a very small staff, their work was excellent and they were loyal and enthusiastic. However, the re-building of our main Weston factory after the fire occupied every minute of my time, and it was the only practical thing to do.

My story of our Scottish activities cannot be complete without reference to all our customers and friends north of the border to all of whom I am so grateful. Twice a year, in the autumn and the spring, my husband and I did our Scottish sales trip.

First we would call on our manufacturers of cloth in the borders, Andrew Stewart and Lochcarron of Galashiels, both of whom wove woollen tweeds and tartans specially for us; Pringle's of Hawick, Kinloch Anderson of Edinburgh and other well-known mills also supplied us. Next we would visit Edinburgh and The Trossachs to discuss our proposed next year's range. Jenners world-famous store with its high quality merchandise; The Tartan Gift Shop, the Fraser Stores, John Knox's House, John Menzies Bookshop and others in Edinburgh; McEwens of Perth and the many beautiful small shops in the Trossachs: Glamis Castle; Inverary Castle (for whom we made special dolls in the Campbell tartan) Braemar; Aberdeen; Inverness; Ullapool and then down the Caledonian Canal. After a few days in Glasgow, we went back south. Nearly all the buyers for the larger stores and the owners of the small gift shops became firm friends over the years. As we were never able to leave the business for a holiday, these annual visits to Scotland became enjoyable breaks to which we looked forward greatly. They were also profitable as we always brought back thousands of pounds worth of orders plus invaluable information about the popular and not so popular models and current market trends. The personal friendship and contact which we had with our customers, particularly those in Scotland, provided a solid foundation for our business which no amount of advertising in the media could ever achieve.

One of our oldest Scottish customers is the world famous store of Jenners. The store is in Princes Street and every year Bill and I would have a Scottish "high tea" in their restaurant. This consisted of fresh fried haddock with chipped potatoes. Accompanying this was a huge pot of tea and a plate piled with scones, cakes, shortbreads and a large plate of bread and butter.

We always sat at the same table, which was in an alcove overlooking Princes Street and the Sir Walter Scott memorial.

In the early days, when we first exhibited at the B.T.M.A. Brighton Toy Fair, one of the first visitors to our stand each year was Jenners' toy buyer, Mr. Gascoigne.

He always used to say that he came to spend his money

Ian Rintoul of Jenners, Edinburgh, holding a model of Pegasus used in the film "Clash of the Titans."

with us first so that he could be sure of having enough of his allocation to select the range he wanted. Our orders must have been minimal compared with orders given to the large toy manufacturers, but it was a gesture which I always appreciated.

Mr. Gascoigne retired some years ago and the buyer now is Ian Rintoul. Ian wrote to me recently stating that he was a long-time admirer of Peggy Nisbet's work and has carried a large range of the dolls set in showcases with settings appropriate to the characters. Ian's interest in "miniatures" stems from his hobby of film production where he specialises in using models and scaled-down versions of the real thing. His films have been shown on BBC2 and ITV channels here in the United Kingdom as well as abroad. He is a great admirer of the American film producer, Ray Harryhausen, expert on animation, who does superb model work in films specialising in trick photography. In the photograph Ian is holding a model of Pegasus, the flying horse of mythology, used in one of Ray Harryhausen's films, "Clash of the Titans."

CHAPTER X

British Exhibition —
Coliseum, New York - June 1962
Jetsell, U.S.A. - 1968

Marjorie Smith-Cox and Peggy Nisbet upon arrival in New York.

One of the most spectacular exhibitions in which I have participated was The British Exhibition organized by the Board of Trade. This took place in the Coliseum, New York, overlooking Central Park.

It was hot in June 1962, I think in the nineties, but in the Coliseum, itself, it was cool and pleasant.

When we agreed to participate in the event, it was decided that it would need two people to look after the stand, because

of the long hours during which the exhibition was open to the public and we could not leave the exhibit unattended. It was decided that Marjorie Smith-Cox, wife of our Chairman, Clifton Smith-Cox, should accompany me.

This was before the days when everyone crossing the Atlantic automatically went by air, so we travelled on RMS "Carinthia," a small but comfortable and luxurious Cunard liner.

We boarded her in Liverpool bound for New York but as soon as we sailed, it was announced that we were going via Greenock in Scotland, then to Montreal, from whence we would have to take a train to New York. I cannot remember now why this change had to be made, but I do know that we had a most enjoyable voyage. We sat at the captain's table and, therefore, had the best of service together with pleasant and interesting travelling companions. Our genial host, Captain Marr, subsequently became Commodore of the Cunard Line.

When Marjorie and I finally arrived in New York we went to the Coliseum and arranged our display on the stand allocated to us. We were on the fifth floor and had been given a small area, but in a magnificent position. We were between the entrance, through which every visitor had to pass, and the " Old English Pub," towards which large numbers of the visitors wended their way.

The exhibition was an unusual one. First, it was larger and more comprehensive than most of those normally organised by the Board of Trade and, secondly, it was mounted to demonstrate to the American people every aspect of our industrial, commercial and social life from machinery to whisky to fashion design and everything in between. It was to be a spectacle and not a trade show. No selling was allowed throughout the whole area with three exceptions (1) coins struck by The Royal Mint at the Exhibition itself; (2) beer and refreshments in "The Old English Pub" and (3) Peggy Nisbet historical dolls.

To this day I have no idea why we were selected for such a prestigious concession. We were able to mount our display exactly as we wished, without any interference, and we were allowed to sell our models during the whole of the time the exhibition was open to the public.

It was a magnificent event. As one approached the Coliseum from Central Park, one heard the blare of trumpets and the band of the Grenadier Guards playing at full strength. Upon reaching the entrance, one was confronted by a white wall extending the length of the building onto which was projected a film of the Regiment of the Grenadier Guards, in their colourful scarlet uniforms and black bearskins, marching to the strains of the band. The guardsmen were life-size, so it was a superb and inspiring sight.

It is so long ago that I have forgotten much of the detail, but the most exciting exhibition of all was a part of the Royal Mint which had been brought over and installed in full working order.

Silver crown pieces were actually minted and sold to the public as they watched and there was a queue from morning to night. I bought some myself and hope that I still have them somewhere amongst all my belongings, although I do not know where.

Whenever I return from a trip I bring back books, catalogues, programmes, souvenirs, maps, postcards, menus, book-matches, dolls, gifts from friends: a hundred and one different things, most of which I carefully pack into cardboard cartons, ready to "go through when I have time." The trouble is, I never do seem to have the time, so I have had to rent two garages in the town, which are stacked high with these and other items I want to keep. One garage alone has 90 large cartons of papers, newspaper cuttings, postcards, and so forth, ready to file and catalogue — one day I will go through them all.

Once, when I visited the English pub at lunchtime, I saw two men sitting there, one of whom had a very familiar face. It was Randolph Churchill, son of Sir Winston Churchill. Amongst the dolls I had taken with me were a number of models of Sir Winston in the robes of the Order of The Garter. I dashed back to my exhibit, got a model off the stand and went back to the pub, which was only a few yards away. With some trepidation, because I felt it was somewhat of an intrusion, I approached Mr. Churchill and proffered him the model saying, "I do hope you will forgive me for interrupting you but do you think, if you were kind enough to take this model home to your father, he would accept it?" He got up, asked me to sit down, and said, "Yes, I am sure he would. How kind of you." We talked for a few minutes and he was most courteous.

Another incident occurred on the same day, strangely enough again in connection with Sir Winston. I was standing alongside our exhibit when an elderly man approached and looked at our display. He then took me to one side and whispered in my ear, "I am just going over to your country to stay with a very important person." I said, " Oh, who is that?" The man was Joyce Hall, the founder of the Hallmark card empire in Kansas City. He told me that every year he went to England to spend a few days with his old friend, Sir Winston, then Mr. Churchill.

Joyce Hall stayed talking to me for some time and then suggested that I should go and see his son-in-law, Robert Marshall, who was at that time president of Hall's Department Store in Kansas City, but who was about to start an import business dealing in high quality gifts, china and glass. He suggested that he might be interested in our dolls. Bob Marshall was married to Joyce Hall's daughter, Barbara, with whose fabulous collection of dolls' houses and miniatures most collectors are familiar.

This was the beginning of a long and happy friendship with Bob and Barbara. After the exhibition closed, I stayed on in the U.S.A. and I went to Kansas City with a range of samples and was welcomed at the Marshall's home. Bob became my importer and distributor in the U.S.A. about which I have written in Chapter XI entitled "Breaking Into the Export Market."

Because of my decision to visit Bob Marshall in Kansas City, we had to change our plans for returning home. Marjorie decided to go back as originally intended, whilst I proceeded to Missouri for my meeting with Bob.

Whilst in New York I called to see the buyers in the leading stores and, most important of all, the buyer at the world famous toy store, F.A. O. Schwarz on Fifth Avenue, who for many years devoted much of their main first floor area to selling our range.

My return passage was booked on the French liner "La Flandre." The sun shone, the sea was calm, and the informal parties at the side of the swimming pool were typically light-hearted and sometimes hilarious. The food and wines were superb. It was a memorable trip.

Jetsell — 1968

Whilst we were exhibiting at the Brighton Toy Fair in February 1968, one of the topics of conversation was a forthcoming sales promotion being launched by *The Daily Express* with the co-operation of the Board of Trade. This was to take place in the U.S.A. and was to be called Jetsell.

Applications were invited from small to medium sized companies who wished to break into the American market, but who had not the finance or expertise to do so on their own. About 50 firms were to be selected.

Several people suggested that I should apply, but I considered that we were too insignificant to qualify and thought no more about it. However, the fair was running smoothly and it suddenly occurred to me that there was no harm in trying; we might have a chance after all.

Upon looking at that morning's *Daily Express*, I found that applications had to be in by midday the following day. At lunch time, when buyers were slowing up, I took a pad, went to my bedroom which was in The Grand Hotel where we were also exhibiting, and wrote an application.

In 1968 our small souvenir dolls, which we were marketing under the name of "Tower Treasures Ltd" in order to differentiate from our more expensive historical range, were becoming very popular, so Alison and I thought we would both send an application to Jetsell. The applicant had to be the managing director or someone in a senior position in the company so we made a joint application. I applied in the name of Peggy Nisbet Ltd, whilst Alison applied in the name of Tower Treasures Ltd.

By this time we had become quite enthusiastic over the project and felt we could not trust the postal service to get our applications to the *Sunday Express* the next day, so Alison held the fort on the stand, whilst I caught a fast early train to London. From the station I took a taxi to the *Daily Express* offices in Fleet Street, kept it waiting whilst I deposited our applications, then returned to Victoria Station and then back to Brighton. I was only away for three hours and was back on the stand before lunch, breathless but excited.

It did not seriously occur to me that we should be chosen, but when the list of successful companies was published in the *Daily Express*, there were our two names. Both companies had been selected, so Alison and I would have each other's company on the trip. It was fortunate that we were both able to go because there was only one other woman on the mission.

Jetsell was to take place in April so we only had one month in which to organise the work at the factory during our absence, and to prepare two ranges of samples.

Everything was done on a luxurious scale. All the participants met at a champagne reception in the V.I.P. lounge at Heathrow, hosted by Max Aitken of the *Daily Express*. We had a VC 10 for our exclusive use and had a most enjoyable flight.

We landed at Boston, and went straight to a briefing, and then to another reception, to which leading industrialists and businessmen had been invited. Board of Trade officials and commercial attachés effected introductions and arranged interviews. We had press and television coverage wherever we went, and a transport plane went ahead of our plane so that our samples were awaiting us at each city when we arrived.

From Boston we went to Atlanta, Washington, D.C., New York, St. Louis, Minneapolis, Toronto and, finally, to Montreal, where we embarked for our return journey to the U.K.

There is so much of interest to relate but, alas, no space in which to tell it.

It was very hard work, but we obtained good orders and many important contacts. Neither Alison nor I had ever been in Miami, and in 1968, when general air travel was in its infancy, a visit to Miami was a very special affair. When Alison and I were in Atlanta we had a spare afternoon, so we took a plane to Miami, hired a car at the airport, rushed to the beach, had a quick swim in the ocean, then dashed back to Atlanta.

On our return journey to England, we had just left Montreal airport when it was announced over the loudspeaker that Martin Luther King had been assassinated. It was only a few days earlier that we ourselves had been in Atlanta.

Peggy Nisbet and Alison Wilson, Miami Beach, 1968.

51

Breaking into Export Markets - 1960s U.S.A., Canada, Australia

There is a great divergence of opinion amongst British manufacturers as to the best way in which to open up a new market overseas. The U.S.A. is, and always has been, our best export market, so I will describe my own experience.

The method of distribution adopted does, of necessity, depend upon the type of merchandise offered, and the potential demand.

My problem was not a difficult one because I knew what a great number of doll collectors there were in the U.S.A. If, then, I were to produce dolls of a sufficiently high quality and of sufficient interest to be acceptable to the doll collector, they would be sought after and would sell themselves: which is exactly what they did.

Instead of advertising in magazines, newspapers and on television, which I could not afford in any case, my idea was to obtain exposure of my dolls to as great an audience of doll collectors as possible. This was easier than might have been expected because my range of characters, consisting as they did of the royal family, historical and other famous characters of the past and present, were of interest to the press and television presenters in connection with current affairs. They used the dolls in their articles and programmes. In fact, they approached me, rather than I approaching them, and it was all free advertising.

The second thing I did, partly to obtain exposure for my models, but equally because of the pleasure derived from personal involvement when I met so many people and learned so much from them, was to accept as many invitations to trade fairs, trade missions and store promotions as came my way.

There are obviously enormous sales to be obtained by advertising a mass produced article on television, but where a handmade or individual product is concerned, I cannot subscribe to the modern method of selling it from a desk by telephone instead of taking the trouble to visit a buyer and taking a selection of samples suitable for that particular shop or outlet. One cannot sell that kind of merchandise by remote control. A customer needs information and inspiration from a salesman in order to work up enthusiasm for a product: in fact, a salesman sells himself as well as his product.

It was not until my own doll was in production, and we were installed in a factory, that it was possible to turn my thoughts to appointing an agent in the U.S.A. All the main London stores were reporting that a large proportion of their sales of Peggy Nisbet dolls were to Americans visiting Britain, so obviously distribution in the States was necessary.

My first step was to visit the London buying offices of American stores. Marshall Field & Co. had their own buying office in London, whilst other U.S. stores were represented by London buying houses such as The Associated Merchandising Corporation and Associated Dry Goods.

For a newcomer like myself this was an ideal situation. It merely meant an occasional visit to London to visit the confirming houses. Sometimes a range of samples was left in their office so that they were readily available for buyers arriving in the U.K. for a few hours only, but usually appointments were made for me to see any visiting buyers, one of whom would frequently buy for a whole group of stores. I would then make a special trip to London and orders always arrived within a short space of time.

This situation existed until, as a result of our participation in trade fairs and other promotions, it became necessary for us to have in the U.S.A. itself not only a sales force but, in addition, an importer/distributor who would sell and also hold stocks in their warehouse in order to give quick deliveries to their customers.

Alas, I do not have the space in this book to mention and describe the agents we appointed on a trial basis. All of them were enthusiastic, hard working and, in their own way, efficient. However, our range was not an easy one to handle, mainly because it was NOT mass produced. Although our turnover was relatively small, any agent who was appointed would have to be in possession of sufficient capital to hold comparatively costly stocks of a large proportion of our large range. From their point of view, therefore, it was not a viable proposition, and many of our earlier arrangements must have meant a great deal of work for small return. Neither was it satisfactory for us to change our representation too often.

The first importer and distributor who handled our dolls in a nationwide, professional way was Bob Marshall of Marshall Imports Inc., Kansas City. There is mention elsewhere in this book of the way in which I met Bob and his wife, Barbara, and how he became our agent.

Bob had a large warehouse in Kansas City and beautiful showrooms in New York and Los Angeles and showed at all the important gift fairs. We met once or twice a year in the U.S.A. or in the U.K. to discuss the range he was carrying, and made plans for the following year. It was a very flexible and happy arrangement. Bob was not demanding and was even prepared to allow us to supply stock orders direct to the leading stores whilst supplying them with "fill-ins" of any items they wanted urgently.

There was one worry. Marshall Imports supplied the

china and glass departments and the gift trade almost exclusively. We, too, had a market in these areas, but we also had a market in toy departments and speciality doll shops upon whom their salesmen did not call.

For some time we carried on as we were because we were not short of orders. However, as our manufacturing capacity increased and I became more and more involved with doll collectors, we decided that as much as we enjoyed our business relationship, we ought to have wider representation.

Bob had always said that if ever we wanted to appoint another agent he would understand and release us from our agreement, so when we were approached by Reeves International, Inc., who had extensive showrooms in the Toy Building, 200 Fifth Avenue, New York, asking if they could represent us, I discussed the matter with Bob, and we agreed that I ought to appoint them.

There were two problems. One was that Jack Wilson was at that time thinking of joining our company and I did not think I should change agents without discussing it with a prospective new colleague. For two months I wrote to Reeves making excuses for not reaching a decision. Then, when Jack did, in fact, join us, we both decided that we should use Reeves and Jack went to see them. I have never regretted that decision.

The second problem was that Reeves was the agent for the well-known Steiff bears and soft toys, so obviously could not represent us in that field. We had by then started to obtain a satisfactory amount of sales in bears which Jack has since built up into a very large Teddy Bear business, but in those early days we decided to continue to sell them ourselves, through the good offices of Phil Rubin in California and other regional distributors, whilst allowing Reeves to market the Peggy Nisbet Collectors' Costume dolls. Reeves did an excellent job.

Led by their President, Mr. Fleischman, they have a superb team headed by Gerry Fisher, assisted by Howard Horii, both of whom I consider to be old and valued friends. I well remember how grateful I was to Howard and his wife, Carol, when I was ill with a heavy cold whilst staying at the Plaza Hotel, New York. They came in and out with flowers, fruit, hot lemon drinks, aspirin and medications — even miniature bottles of brandy, to speed my recovery. When one is thousands of miles from home and not well, this kind of thoughtfulness is appreciated.

Most of all, however, the one individual I have to thank for the success and pleasure of my tours is Bob Moynihan. Reeves has a sales team stretching over the length and breadth of the States. Robert Moynihan joined them as sales manager in 1974, after holding various positions with Jordan Marsh,

Child World and Vogue Dolls. He was born in Boston, graduated from Northeastern University in 1962 and received his Masters Degree in Business Administration from Boston University in 1969. Over the years we developed a pleasant and enjoyable business relationship based, for my part, on extreme gratitude for his thoughtfulness and cheerfulness. Nothing was too much trouble and if I asked for any alteration to my itinerary, he would always reply with a twinkle in his eyes, "No problem!" He is an avid sports fan, his special love being thoroughbred racing. With the thousands of miles he travelled every week, I do not know how he found time to marry, but marry he did. Kathy is attractive, vivacious and very good company. They have a lovely apartment in New York. Bob took the trouble to come and see me at every store I attended. He made sure they had stocks of dolls to back up the promotion and, on one occasion, even fetched some from New York himself by air when the store ran out of dolls.

In Minneapolis, Reeves is represented by Ted Cook. He, his wife, Martha, and his son, Gary, have also become friends over the years. It is always a joy to see Ted's smiling face greeting me at the airport and a pleasure, too, to visit him and his family at their home. Martha insists on calling me "Peg," the only one of my friends to do so.

We were fortunate with our other overseas agents.

There is one more of "Reeves' men," as they are called, to whom I am particularly indebted. Ken Kuehn and his wife, Martha, live in Los Angeles and Ken represents the area for Reeves. He helped me when I was at Robinsons Store in Beverly Hills and drove me to San Diego where I was at Bullocks Store for a short time.

We were so near the Mexican border that I said to Ken, "I did not realise how very close we are to Mexico. I should love to see just a little of it." He said, "Martha and I often spend a weekend in Ensenada. Why don't we all go down at the weekend?"

It was a glorious break and I enjoyed the wonderful scenery. Mexico had just devalued its currency and I bought a lovely bracelet, ring and ear-rings made by a well-known jeweller/artist who designed his own pieces. They were made of the traditional Mexican silver, copper and turquoise and I wear the set constantly.

We stayed in a beautiful little hotel with white walls and verandahs from which flowers of brilliant colours cascaded into the courtyard below.

The only disturbing moments were when crossing the border. It was shocking to see the dramatic change from the affluence of California to the poverty of Mexico — only a few miles, and such a change in peoples and their way of life.

CANADA

Our agent in Canada is Austin Lambe who operates as Austin Lambe Imports Ltd., Box 298, Alexandria, K0C 1A0.

Recently I wrote to Austin, asking him if he would let me have a few notes about our association over the years. Instead of paraphrasing his report, I am including his letter in its entirety.

Austin has always been the most courteous and dedicated of agents. He is quiet, intelligent, thoughtful and knows his job inside out. Thankfully, he is not the aggressive type of salesman so prevalent, alas, to-day, but he looks after his customers and principals, thus preserving a continuity of business which he has provided for us over several decades. It is good, solid "bread and butter" business, with no traumatic

ups and downs, producing a steady flow of orders throughout the year from carefully selected stockists. During World War II Austin left the university and enlisted. In 1943 he came to England with the Canadian forces, was wounded in France, and met his future wife, Bea, also a Canadian, who had come over to Europe as a nurse.

The sales trips upon which I accompanied Austin were most enjoyable and instructive, as also were the trade fairs, but I attended so few, from sheer lack of time. I wish it had been possible for me to attend more, but my Canadian tours were, of necessity, tied up with my U.S. trips, so my choice was limited, and there was not enough time to do more.

Canada is an interesting market which deserved far more attention than I was ever able to devote to it. Austin was

Austin Lambe.

always suggesting special models to be made exclusively for the country, some of which I designed and produced but there were many more interesting subjects that I never got around to making. Austin deserved more backing than I was able to give him, particularly as the number of doll collectors in Canada is increasing rapidly.

After my last trip to Toronto I wanted to see the Rockies, so I took a plane to Calgary, then spent a day at Banff Springs. The scenery defies description. From there I caught the train with the observation coach which runs to Vancouver. I took dozens of photographs but they do not do justice to the wonderful views. When I am old and decrepit I shall put these in albums and see them again with my "inner eye."

AUSTIN LAMBE IMPORTS LTD.

BOX 298, ALEXANDRIA ONT. K0C 1A0

PHONE: (613) 525-4143   2 Sep 86

Peggy Nisbet
c/o House of Nisbet Ltd.
Avon BS25 1AG
England.

Dear Peggy,

It was a real delight to hear you speaking on the phone the other day. I recognized the voice at once.

You asked me to find a photograph of myself for use in your forthcoming book. I assumed that could be a simple procedure but in fact I have turned the house inside out before finding this one enclosed. Just where all the family snapshots are filed, framed or mounted is yet to be discovered and the blame is mine, I am told, for not packing them properly when the household was moved three years ago. But I did find this gem which was taken in a show in Montreal, in Place Boneventure. And I could add that the pipe is no longer a fixture; I am now in my ninth month without that pacifier and, I think, I am performing very nicely.

The visits you made to Canada in your early effort to establish the Nisbet line are interesting for recall now because the years do slide by. Your first trip was by ocean liner to Montreal, on a Cunarder, I think the Carinthia or a sister ship. You had a full day of steaming up the St. Lawrence before docking in Montreal. Those were the days before flying across the ocean was established. And that was the time you had a small Mountie doll in your pocket, part of the Happy Doll group, -ready for business as always. This was the time we drove to Quebec City along the old winding roads. Perhaps you remember the persistent storm which followed us home to Montreal that night.

A year or so after that introduction you were back in Montreal showing your line in a U.K. trade exhibit. I think that was the time we made the long drive trip through Toronto and Hamilton and beyond to Niagara Falls where we had at that time an excellent display of the Nisbet originals. It is interesting to observe now that many of those original numbers are still in the Nisbet line.

Peggy, I think these are the highlights you wanted me to recall and my hope is that this small contribution helps in your project. Bea sends her love. She has been on duty over the week-end as grandmother to her fourth grandchild, a one-year-old named Andrew.

With all kind thoughts, Peggy,

Sincerely,

AUSTRALIA

In Australia we are represented by Crown & Andrews Pty Ltd of 36 Cowper Street, Granville, N.S.W. 2142 (Sketch-a-Graph Pty Ltd).

Their set-up is very different from the Canadian agency. The company was formed in 1957 when Vic Andrews and Gerry Crown arrived in Australia from the U.K. Their speciality was demonstrating, and in their early years they used to demonstrate in the Meyer and other department stores, selling mainly kitchen gadgets.

By 1963 they had expanded and started to advertise their products on television and in 1967 they introduced their most famous product, Sketch-a-Graph. As a result of their success with this item, they decided to concentrate almost entirely on the toy trade, handling high quality toys and games.

Audrey New, their Marketing Director, teamed up with Gerry Crown over 12 years ago. They were a formidable team. There were virtually no women executives in the Australian toy industry, so Audrey set out to become the first. By diligence and, I suspect, a natural flair, she became a leading executive, in addition to which she did so much philanthropic work that she earned the title of the Charity Queen of the Toy Industry.

Audrey did not achieve her executive position of Marketing Director easily — she first of all completed a rough four-year management course at Meadowbrook Technical College, where she was the only woman student.

At trade fairs she is indefatigable, always on the alert, looking for items of quality and interest.

Audrey formed the Peggy Nisbet Doll Collectors' Club of Australia, which was based on the club I formed during my visit to Stewarts of Baltimore in 1954.

Jerry Crown and Audrey New.

Peggy Nisbet
Doll
Collectors' Club
Australia

Your Membership No. is: _____

P.O. BOX 154, BURWOOD N.S.W. 21:
TELEPHONE 745.319

AUSTRALIAN NEWSHEET NO. 1

Dear Club Member,

This is the first of our Australian Newsheets and I think it would be a good idea to introduce myself and then tell you how I am planning our club and what my aims and objectives are.

I am thirty-nine years old - forty in October - and married with a seventeen year old daughter. My job is General Manager and Sales Manager for Crown & Andrews a toy importing and exporting firm. My previous experience include three years in the Navy and also working in France for NATO. It was has been as an Executive Private Secretary and I have had various jobs which my travels that made me first interested in dolls and when Crown & Andrews were able to obtain the Peggy Nisbet Doll Agency for Australia I was overjoyed, because now I could mix business with pleasure by forming an Australian branch of the Peggy Nisbet Doll Collectors' Club.

As you know, the Peggy Nisbet Dolls are among the most superb dolls in the world. In this day of mass production and symmetry it is nearly impossible to own a unique objet d'art without spending practically a fortune in order to do so. These lovely dolls, however, are painted by hand and the clothes are all stitched by skilled ladies working in their own homes and at their own pace under no pressures. In this way each doll becomes an individual piece, put together with love and care.

Collecting dolls, like collecting anything, is an expanding hobby. Expanding not only in numbers of dolls a collector eventually owns but expanding in knowledge and understanding of history and people.

This is where I would like to see the Doll Collectors Club Australia fit in. Doll Collectors are a select group of people and normally one doesn't find too many of one's closest friends interested in the hobby. Therefore I think it would be very nice if I could try to bring everyone together, in some small way at least.

As I see it, by the media of this newsheet and interchange of ideas and articles from the members, I can bring together the collectors in the different localities. This is just a nucleus of an idea and I would love to receive letters from the Members and have your ideas of how we can expand the club and so gain a lot of mutual pleasure. So please do write to me so that I can publish your letters for everyone to read and enjoy.

/....

PEGGY NISBET DOLL COLLECTORS' CLUB

- 2 -

Australia has been a little neglected in the past and I hope that we will now gain more collectors and more interest in this fascinating hobby.

You have seen the list of stockists of the Peggy Nisbet Dolls and I hope that this list will continue to grow. Myers are most interested in the Peggy Nisbet Dolls and their big city stores are all putting in a permanent exhibition, so please go along and see them and talk to the assistants in the stores who will be happy to talk to you and take what orders you wish to leave with them.

I had the pleasure of visiting the Peggy Nisbet offices in Weston-Super-Mare, England, while I was over there at the toy fairs earlier this year. I also had luncheon with Peggy at her delightful home which is a converted water tower on a hill in Weston-Super-Mare not far from the beach. She intends to put a swimming pool on the roof one day. How exciting it all is!

As I have said, please write to me so that I can publish your letters.

I hope you also enjoy the latest International Newsletter which is enclosed.

Yours sincerely,

Audrey A. New.

P.S. Crown and Andrews have a thrilling offer for you. Details enclosed.

AAN.

ABOVE — BACKGROUND: Glastonbury Scene.

ABOVE — DOLLS: Special Collectors Set No. 11: LE/69 *King Arthur;* LE/70 *Queen Guinevere;* LE/72 *Lady Anne;* LE/73 *Lady Sybil.*

LEFT: H/264 *Queen Guinevere* (early standard model).

St. Paul's Cathedral.

BELOW: Characters from the film "Oliver": Fagin, Artful Dodger, Nancy, Mr. Bumble, Bill Sykes and Oliver Twist.

BOTTOM LEFT: BR/315 Pearly Queen; BR/314 Pearly King.

BOTTOM RIGHT: Cries of London: BR/304 Lavender Girl; BR/309 Flower Girl; BR/307 Turnips and Carrots Ho!

ABOVE: H/227 Madame Pompadour; H/215 Queen Marie Antoinette; H/371 Madame du Barry.

RIGHT: P/461 Josephine Beauharnais and P/460 Napoleon Bonaparte.

BELOW: Special Collectors Set No. 7: P/694 Anne of Austria; LE/54 Madame de Maintenon; LE/50 King Louis XIV (Sun King); LE/53 Marquise de Montespan.

P/602 Katherine of Aragon; P/603 Anne Boleyn; P/604 Jane Seymour; P/605 Anne of Cleves; P/606 Catherine Howard; P/607 Catherine Parr; H/218 King Henry VIII.

P/603 Anne Boleyn and H/217 Anne Boleyn.

H/217 Anne Boleyn; H/222 Anne of Cleves; H/223 Catherine Parr; H/219 Katherine of Aragon; H/221 Catherine Howard; H/220 Jane Seymour; H/218 King Henry VIII.

View of Wells Cathedral.

P/821 *Pope John Paul* and P/797 *Pope John XXIII.*

**Special Collectors Set No. 17: Limited edition of 500 sets: LE/93 *Cardinal Wolsey;*
LE/91 *King Henry VIII* (Field of the Cloth of Gold); LE/92 *Catherine of Aragon.***

ABOVE — BACKGROUND: View
of Axbridge.

ABOVE — DOLLS: Special collectors Set
No. 14: LE/80 *Eleanor of Aquitaine* (1976);
LE/79 *King Richard I*; LE/82 *Standard
Bearer*; LE/81 *Queen Berengaria*.

H/566 Baron of King John's Court; H/567 Baron's Lady; H/299 King John.

View of Bath. A Regency Terrace.

Regency Group.

Uniforms: Top: BR/317 *Guardsman*; BR/320 *London Policeman*; B/330 *Yeoman Warder (Beefeater)*; Y/1000 *Yeoman Warder of the Tower of London (Beefeater)*. Bottom: BR/321 *Household Cavalry (Life Guards)*; BR/322 *Household Cavalry (The Blues)*; K/4 *Piper*; BR/325 *Black Watch Piper*.

CHAPTER XII

More Trade Fairs
—————1960s and 1970s—————

For some years the only fairs we attended were those organised by the toy industry. Our existing order books kept us busy, but now we were in a factory and had our new dolls; we felt the time was ripe to show our range more extensively.

It had become apparent that we had a far wider market than in the toy shops and the toy departments of stores so we decided to take space at the International Gift Fair which was held annually in Blackpool.

This event was held in the Winter Gardens which is the Leisure Centre of the town during the summer months. It consisted of a very large building divided into various sections, which included a ballroom, a theatre, a vast basement or lower floor and a wide balcony which, in summer held tables and chairs for light refreshments. When the gift fair was held, these were all divided up into stands, some in the ballroom and others in the theatre. Our stand was always on the balcony. In later years the International Gift Fair has been held at the National Exhibition Centre in Birmingham, which is perhaps more conventional but not nearly so much fun.

Our decision was more than justified and gift buyers from all over the country placed orders, mainly for the tourist and high class gift trades. At our first gift fair an enterprising and athletic press photographer persuaded me to take a set of *Henry VIII* and *His Six Wives* to the sea front overlooking the bay. He placed the group on the promenade and then proceeded to lie down flat on his face with his camera resting on the ground. He took some beautiful photographs which appeared in the local and national press showing *Henry* and his entourage walking along the Blackpool Prom!

The size of the orders astounded me, and at our first gift fair we exceeded anything that we had ever taken at the toy fairs. Buyers bought our small *Happy Doll* range for monthly deliveries throughout the whole of the tourist season: hundreds of *Pipers* for the Edinburgh Festival, *Scottish Dancers* for the Highland Games, and *Musselburgh Fisherwomen*, in addition to models in the *Campbell Tartan* made exclusively for the Duke of Argyll's Souvenir Shop at Inverary Castle; *Boy* and *Girl Dancers* for the Aboyne Games, all in authentic miniature tartans; and a large number of other "specials," the list of which increased each year.

These souvenir Scottish dolls sold in very large quantities. They were more expensive than other types on the market, but the tartans were 100% wool and the costumes well made and accurate; they were very good value for money.

In the more expensive ranges we had *Highland Chieftains*, *Mary Queen of Scots* and a *Peatgatherer* which is still one of my favourite dolls. The face was specially modelled with the high cheekbones of the highlander. The *Peatgatherers*' dark brown dresses were made of 100% fine wool cloth, and we made

handknitted black shawls to go round their shoulders. The Scots are very proud of their country and their skills, and they were pleased to have a doll which was a genuine Scottish product.

Buyers at the Blackpool Fair were not all from Scotland. From London we had large orders for guardsmen, policemen and beefeaters. Very few of the gift buyers attend the toy fairs, so they had not seen our range. The Gift Association also ran fairs at Torquay and Harrogate, and after our success at Blackpool we exhibited at these each year, with excellent results.

Gradually, as our manufacturing capacity increased, we became more ambitious. At the toy and gift fairs we saw, and obtained orders from buyers from several of the large U.S.A. stores, but not every buyer comes to the U.K. The B.T.M.A. took space each year at two of the largest overseas fairs in New York and Nurnberg. This space was divided into small sections and allocated to members if they wished to participate. They were partly subsidised by the Board of Trade.

There is not sufficient space to describe all our adventures, but one or two episodes are worthy of mention.

My first New York Toy Fair was full of difficulties. Air travel was not in general use, so I travelled by sea on one of the Cunard liners. The days leading up to my departure were hectic. Samples and stands had been despatched weeks earlier in a container with the samples of all the other British exhibitors, but there were last minute prototypes I was taking with me, and other items omitted from the container. Once on board, however, I had five days in which to collect myself and make preparations for the fair.

Once we landed though, my troubles started. Despite all the enquiries we had made and instructions which has been supplied to us, all of which we dutifully followed, the U.S. Customs authorities refused to accept my documents for clearance of the samples, which could not be found in any case because they had arrived before me, and no-one knew where they were. I was at the docks for hours. Finally, British Embassy and B.T.M.A. officials tracked them down. The fair was being held at the Statler Hotel, New York, where I also had a bedroom reserved for me, so at last I was able to relax.

The fair was very successful, and whilst I was in the States I took the opportunity of visiting stores on the East Coast with whom I was already doing business through their London confirming houses. Taking the Amtrak service I visited Wannamakers in Philadelphia; Garfinckels and Woodward & Lothrop in Washington; Stewarts in Baltimore; Jordan Marsh in Boston and obtained orders from them all. In New York I visited, amongst many others, F.A.O. Schwarz, which in later years carried large displays of our dolls covering one entire wall near their Fifth Avenue entrance; Bloomingdales, B. Altmans, Saks Fifth Avenue, Macys - all of them were interested, and most placed orders.

The Nurnberg Toy Fair, to which buyers and exhibitors come from all over the world, was our next overseas trade fair. We were a very small company, but even the large ones only had enough room to exhibit a token range of samples. Nevertheless, it was instructive, and was our first venture into the European market.

Our Chairman and his wife, Clifton and Marjorie Smith-Cox, came with me to have a look at this most famous of all international fairs.

The toy association was exhibiting under the auspices of the Board of Trade, and our group was heavily subsidised by the British government. The fair was mainly to "fly the flag" and to establish whether British manufacturers could compete with the world's leading producers of toys. We did not get many orders, but it was an excellent fact-finding trip, which was helpful when planning our future Nurnberg fairs.

Fortunately, we took with us Brigitte Charsley, who is German born, and was therefore a perfect colleague. She has been a member of our staff for several years so knew all about our dolls, and was particularly helpful on the stand as an interpreter. We were able to find sources of supply for many accessories, particularly diamante stones and miniature items of different kinds, which were unobtainable in the U.K.

Our second Nurnberg Fair was chaotic. I took Brigitte with me again, and we went on our own because by this time we knew the procedures. When we arrived, we learned that a new Exhibition Centre was being built, but that until it was completed the fair was being held in temporary premises. These premises consisted of a series of tents with duckboards as floors, placed loosely over squelching mud. It was freezing, with several inches of snow, and heaters blowing blasts of hot air from all quarters. There were outside toilets housed in a wooden hut and supervised by a grim witch-like woman dressed in black who thrust out her hand each time we appeared, demanding payment of some ridiculously high sum for the privilege of using the lavatories. Since we drank innumerable cups of coffee and refreshing white wine to counteract the stuffy atmosphere, the expenditure on toilets became quite heavy.

The day after we arrived we went to inspect our stand, expecting to see our samples in tea-chests ready to be unpacked. Alas! Lufthansa Airways had decided to have a strike and our samples were stranded at Hanover. We tried to collect them by road, but could not get them released. Many of the exhibitors had brought their samples by road from England in their own vehicles so they were alright, but we could do nothing but sit and wait.

Opening day came, but still no samples. We put up a large notice on our stand, "No samples due to Lufthansa Strike, Please come back later," and sat in front of it, talking to and taking names and addresses of potential buyers to whom we promised to send price lists and catalogues. I pestered the organisers, the British Commercial Attache, the Lufthansa offices, the transport company the B.T.M.A. officials. We had meetings because other exhibitors were also without their samples, but all our efforts proved fruitless. On the third day the tea-chests arrived, and at long last we were able to put up our display. It was a disheartening experience.

Our third Nurnberg Fair was very different. It was to be the first fair ever held in the newly built Exhibition Centre. This time Alison and Brigitte both came with me as we had a large stand and numbers of buyers from nearly every country in the world were expected to attend. When the three of us arrived at the airport, the snow was lying thick on the ground and it was bitterly cold, but although the temperature was low, it was such a dry cold after the English damp winter weather that we felt exhilarated rather than uncomfortable. We had planned to get to Nurnberg two days before the opening to ensure that we had plenty of time to find our samples and arrange the display.

There was a special bus running to the Exhibition Centre, so we caught it and duly disembarked, then stood transfixed. There in front of us was an attractive building, but in the foreground were several bulldozers on what appeared to be a rough building site. Inside was chaos. Sanitary equipment, wash-basins, lavatories and disconnected telephones were strewn all over the floor of the entrance hall. Workmen were hammering and fixing all kinds of equipment and it seemed impossible that a fair could be held there in 48 hours time.

There was one bit of consolation - our samples and stand fixtures had duly arrived. All we could do, however, was to go back to our hotel, have a good meal and hope for the best.

When we went to erect and dress the stand the next day, wonders had been performed. We were able to take possession of our stand, put up our samples and get everything ready for the opening ceremony the next day. The approach to the Exhibition Centre was still like a building site and I wondered what the buyers, who would be coming from all over the world, would think of it.

Brigitte, Alison and buyer at the Nurnberg Toy Fair, 1973.

Next day was opening day. We arrived at the Exhibition Centre early, and were again transfixed, but this time with admiration. The transformation scene was unbelievable. There were well-constructed, neat and tidy paths, flower beds laid out beautifully with shrubs and trees, flags fluttering in the breeze, with everything swept and garnished: a magnificent sight.

Entrance gates had been installed, telephones were working and toilets were in action. We simply could not believe that so much could have been done in so short a time.

The fair was vast, with hundreds of exhibitors and thousands of buyers. There were magnificent displays including one very large hall devoted entirely to railway lines and electric trains, all running madly on their tracks, flashing by miniature railway stations, villages, woods and tiny little porters and passengers. It was a wonderful sight. As there were three of us, one was often able to leave the stand and see the other exhibits. I particularly liked the German dolls and the exquisite Austrian crafts. In the evenings we ate at a different restaurant each night, then went on to the Cafe Krölle, a lovely building on a balcony overlooking The Square. On the ground floor was a mouth-watering display of cakes, biscuits, chocolates and sweets from which ascended a wide elegant wrought-iron staircase with polished brass handrails. This led to a gallery with small tables at which were served hot chocolate and coffee brimming with cream and ice cream, all accompanied by tiered plates of delicious cream pastries and cakes. It was a meeting place for all of us relaxing after a tiring day.

Nurnberg is a very tiring fair, mainly because it is so vast and has so many participants and visitors. It is, however, so interesting that the hours fly past.

So many unexpected enquiries are made, some of which lead to future business, but all of which are instructive. Fairs are not judged merely by the orders taken on the stand. There are the contacts made, the information gained, and the whole atmosphere which generates new ideas and makes one think.

No great orders were ever taken by us at Nurnberg, but it is a market place that cannot be ignored.

We have never done a great volume of business in France other than with the large Parisian stores Au Printemps, Trois Quartiers and, of course, Au Nain Bleu, but when we were invited by the Board of Trade to participate in the Foire de Lyon, we accepted with alacrity.

The Foire de Lyon is a large fair consisting of every kind of commodity. In addition to our toy section there were exhibits ranging from gifts to heavy machinery and farm implements, plus, of course, wine: barrels, casks, bottles of red, white, rosé, table wines and wine of every description.

Dexam International had asked if they could act as our agents and we agreed that they should represent us on a one year's trial basis. We discussed which models to exhibit and decided that our souvenir range of military uniforms would be of most interest, in addition to which it would make an eye-catching and colourful display. We, therefore, took with us guardsmen, pipers, London policemen, drummers, yeoman warders of The Tower of London (beefeaters) together with a background made to represent the Horse Guards Parade, where the Queen holds the Trooping The Colour ceremony each year in June.

We had been advised to take samples in under the "Carnet" system. This meant that we would not have to pay duty when they entered France, on condition that we brought them all back to the U.K. after the fair.

All went well and we had a superb stand in the main aisle of the Exhibition Centre. We had taken literally dozens of guardsmen with us, and Michael Fox, who accompanied me, arranged them in battalions on the sand coloured ground. The effect was magnificent and we were congratulated by our fellow exhibitors.

The next morning we went to look at the stand before we started on a tour of the town because the fair was not due to open until the following day. When we got to the stand, we could not believe our eyes. Not one doll remained. Only the Horse Guards Parade stood there - empty.

Then began a nightmare which is still fresh in my mind. Police, fair officials, embassy officials, and officials of all kinds surrounded us, all jabbering away, with crowds of the other exhibitors gathering around giving advice. The gendarmes took us to a little hut where they had their temporary headquarters and interrogated us for hours. My French is good enough to carry on a reasonable conversation but I was not familiar with many of the business and legal phrases. The fair was to open the next morning and there we were again, as in Nurnberg, with an empty stand.

I telephoned the factory and told them to send replacement dolls by air immediately, and to contact the Board of Trade who would liaise with embassy officials in the commercial attache's office in order to cut some of the red tape and ensure our samples got to us. I was doing the same in Lyon.

The gendarmes were very helpful and anxious for us to get our dolls because they and the fair oficials had been responsible for security and it was bad publicity for the fair. News of the theft was flying around so everything was done to assist us.

I cannot remember just how the dolls finally arrived, but arrive they did. Our stand was greatly admired and always surrounded by crowds of people. M. Pompidou stopped at our stand. He complimented us on the display and shook hands.

It was a lovely exhibition. We had excellent accommodations overlooking the river. The weather was cold but sunny, with bright blue skies. The restaurants were magnificent. We had breakfast each morning at a small cafe called "Chez Rose" and one evening had one of the most wonderful meals I have ever eaten, at Leon de Lyon. I am very fond of good food and this was superb. Their specialité, a saucisson de Lyon, was only the commencement of a meal such as I have never had since - and I have been to most of the best restaurants in Britain and the U.S.A. Upon arrival Michael and I found one red rose with a long stem, laid at an angle across a royal blue linen napkin with a matching tablecloth. There were lovely wines and above all was the moment when the aroma of the saucisson reached us as the lid was taken off the hen-shaped cream coloured casserole and a slice cut off the 5in (13cm) diameter sausage. It was a wonderful gastronomic experience. One day I will return. My great grandfather was a Valois, whose family came from Lyon, but he was ostracised and cut off by his family because he married an Englishwoman, my great grandmother. Their daughter, Henriette Valois, was my grandmother.

The finale to the theft of our samples was no less dramatic. Michael and I packed them in Lyon, but - you can guess what came next. We had taken the first set of samples into France on a "Carnet" document, which meant that we had to produce the same samples for customs on the way out. There were, of course, no samples to produce as they had been stolen. It took weeks to sort out the mess. Trade fairs have their problems!

The Fire
——1970——

When we discuss any kind of event in connection with the company, it is always described as "Before the Fire" or "After the Fire," rather as one would say B.C. or A.D.

On 14th May 1970, I had 'flu and was confined to the house. This was an unusual occurrence in itself because I was rarely ill and was always at the factory from 8:30 a.m. until long after all the staff had left in the evening. However, at 5:40 p.m. on this fateful day, I was sitting in my chair at home working on some new models, when the 'phone rang. It was one of my staff, a quiet retiring girl. She said, in a slow and perfectly unemotional voice, "Mrs. Nisbet, I think the factory is on fire. I have just seen smoke coming out of the building." I shouted at her, "Well, get off the 'phone and let me call the fire brigade," which I proceeded to do, but they had already been alerted by several people in the area. My 'flu symptoms vanished as I tore down to the factory, to be met by a sight I shall never forget.

Although I arrived only about ten minutes after the fire was discovered, the whole building was ablaze. Flames were shooting high into the sky and black smoke billowed out in every direction.

My first thought was that some of the staff might have been trapped inside, but I was assured by onlookers, and subsequently by the firemen, that the building was empty.

The factory normally closed at 5:30 p.m. and I was told that everyone had left on time except three employees, one being my Design Assistant, Mabel Perry, who always used to check that everything was in order before she left.

Mrs. Perry has a son, John, who was on the staff of British Petroleum Company in London. On this particular day he had decided to come to Weston to pay a surprise visit to his mother. Having arrived at his home and found it raining, he drove to the factory to pick up his mother. He arrived there about 5:45 p.m. and saw some smoke inside the back of the building. With great presence of mind he immediately took off his jacket, wrapped it round his hand, and smashed the large plate glass window near the stairs down which his mother, entirely oblivious of her danger, was leisurely descending. Black smoke was creeping towards her, but she had not noticed it. In a few minutes she would have been suffocated, and I have no doubt that she owes her life to her son's quick thinking. John dragged her through the window to the courtyard outside. Two girls had been following her downstairs. Onlookers dashed in and pulled them through the gap in the window. All three were taken to hospital suffering from shock and the effects of smoke but, fortunately, they were otherwise unharmed. A few minutes later the fire brigade arrived, but already the fire had taken a strong hold and the whole building was ablaze. When I arrived, it was at its peak and it was obvious that everything would be destroyed.

The Fire, 1970.

Only a miracle enabled me to survive. My private office was a small room under the stairs. Every evening, after the staff had left, I would work there, quietly, before going home. Had I not been home with 'flu, I would have been in that room and it is quite certain that it would have been enveloped in smoke before I had any knowledge of what was happening. I could not possibly have escaped as my office had no outside window. Most of my original models and prototypes were in a large walk-in cupboard leading off my office, together with

Reward: £1,000 to see Nisbet doll

● **Mrs Kenyon with the original doll 58, and Mr Wilson with the replica.**

FOR the sheer pleasure of inspecting and photographing the first doll made by Peggy Nisbet 32 years ago, world famous English dollmaker House of Nisbet Ltd is paying a reward of £1,000 to a collector who lives in upstate New York.

The doll was one of 250 similar models made in 1953 on the strength of a first order for the entire lot from Harrods in London.

The doll was a dressed porcelain model of the Queen in coronation robes made by Peggy Nisbet to commemorate that year's coronation.

House of Nisbet's chairman, Mr Jack Wilson, has flown out to the United States to meet the overjoyed doll collector, Mrs Shirley Kenyon. The doll will return with him on a temporary return visit for inspection and photography at the firm's West Country workrooms in Winscombe.

Explaining the background story which made his "find" so important, Mr Wilson said: "Our company burned to the ground in 1970 and all our archives were lost.

"We have been searching for more than a decade for a collector who possessed a model of this first limited edition.

"A number of search notices appeared in our international collectors' club newsletter, and a few years ago Harrods very helpfully circulated their charge account customers to try and find the elusive doll, all to no avail."

In January of this year Jack Wilson announced the £1,000 reward, on the occasion of Nisbet's introduction of a replica edition. Mrs Kenyon read about it, recognised the similarity between a picture of the replica doll and her original and quickly sent a photograph of hers to Nisbet's Winscombe headquarters.

On the bone china base her number was 58.

Travels

Shirley Kenyon and her husband Edwin live in Alexandria Bay, a beautiful resort on the St Lawrence Seaway in the heart of The Thousand Islands.

Her serious interest in doll collecting began in the 1950s when her daughter was a youngster. The Kenyons would often buy a doll on their travels.

Today Mrs Kenyon's collection contains over 20 Nisbet dolls. Ironically, she was unaware that her Coronation doll was a Peggy Nisbet doll, let alone an elusive original. She bought it about five years ago as part of a collection of 35 a friend was selling before retiring.

The Nisbet original was in this collection but it had long since lost its identification. Jack Wilson said it had also lost its overdress and the orb and sceptre.

Nisbet's chairman said another interesting facet of the story was the way it illustrated how development of Nisbets had come full circle in 30 years.

The original Peggy Nisbet doll was made in the form of a figurine in fine bone china. This was, in fact, the first and last bone china doll made by Nisbet until 1980 when Jack Wilson was the "architect" of a joint doll-making project with England's foremost pottery, Royal Doulton.

"We brought together the ceramic and hand-painting skills of Royal Doulton and the costume design and needlework skills of the House of Nisbet," said Mr Wilson.

"In the world of doll-making the working partnership of Royal Doulton and Nisbet is unique. I regard the Royal Doulton project as a renaissance in the design and manufacture of high quality bone china dolls for today's serious collector."

Before leaving Alexandria Bay, Mr Wilson presented Shirley Kenyon with reg'd No 58 of Nisbet's replica edition of the first Nisbet doll to go with her No 58 of the original series.

The replica edition doll was accompanied by a Nisbet collectors' teddy bear called Gordon Blue. "Gordon Blue is one of our Zodiac Bears," said Mr Wilson, "and he was born under Mrs Kenyon's Zodiac Sign which is Taurus."

my patterns and records and they were, of course, all destroyed.

I usually worked at home at weekends so, fortunately, I have a small number of original models and records which survived, but they are very few.

The entire building, with all its contents, was completely demolished. Only one girder remained, wedged at an angle against the next building.

When an investigation took place the next day to try and find out the cause of the fire, the fire officer said that he thought there must have been a small fracture in a waste pipe which was situated inside the building. It was raining that evening and the rain-water must have seeped onto the electric wiring nearby, causing a short circuit which started the fire.

For us the disaster was of the greatest magnitude. Not only was the building destroyed, but also all our stock of dolls, costmes, materials, patterns and prototypes. All our records were gone. We did not even know what orders were on our books; what money we owed or what was owed to us. We did not know the names and addresses of our customers or suppliers, or even our outworkers.

The next morning we had a meeting at my house. Neither the chairman of the company nor my family thought I would ever start the business again, but I was determined not to have all my years of hard work and development destroyed by a fire. I made up my mind to build up the business again, however difficult it might be.

The fire took place on Thursday, 14th May 1970. On Friday, May 15th, after seeing the fire brigade and other officials, I sat down at a telephone in my home and called all our main suppliers whose names I could remember. They were all marvellous. The support I had from them was beyond belief.

My first call was to the managing director of the company that moulded our dolls - by an amazing bit of luck all our moulds were at their factory because we had recently sent them a moulding order upon which they were working. Had the moulds been in our own factory, we could not have re-started production for many months because they would all have been destroyed, and it would have taken six months or more to get new ones made. Our company could not have survived.

Mr. Dunkley, the Managing Director of Mornings Limited, who moulded all our dolls, got in his men over the weekend and on Monday, 18th May, he sent a van down to Weston with a consignment of dolls. I can never thank him enough for his help and his promptitude in assisting us, not only at the time of the fire, but throughout the whole of our business association.

Singer Sewing Machine Company brought us six sewing machines by special delivery in their own van the following Monday and installed them on the ground floor of The Tower, which we had been using as a store.

Patterns that were with outworkers whom we could contact were collected and duplicates made, so that we did not stop production for one day and not one single employee was laid off. The staff were marvellous, as were our suppliers. Bales of materials arrived daily.

So there I was, back at square one and with a challenge which I could not ignore. This challenge was to provide me with first and foremost hard work, to the exclusion of any personal social life, other than business functions and, secondly, with a personal financial burden from which I have never fully recovered. From the business angle we were underinsured. The value of the building had increased, but we had not increased the insurance cover. In addition, we were inadequately covered for our "loss of profits" on what was a rapidly expanding business. These were oversights by our advisers which, with hindsight, ought not to have occurred. It made life very difficult over the ensuing years when we had to re-build the business on a shoestring.

However, we survived and we continued to grow, although I could not pursue the many plans I had made for future development due to lack of capital.

CHAPTER XIV

Rising from the Ashes

―1970―

With the business expanding and with no premises, records, materials or orders, something had to be done, and with my loyal staff, we proceeded to rebuild the Peggy Nisbet doll making business.

My own home again became the hub of the business and we turned one bedroom into a cutting room-cum-general work-room, another into an office, with every square inch occupied by bales of materials, boxes of ribbons and braids, together with dolls, paints and all the items required for production. The sewing machines were installed in The Tower and my sitting room was full of files and dressed dolls. We rented a basement flat nearby which we used as a packing department and a store for our display cartons and packing cases. It was all very time-consuming and inconvenient, but we managed.

When looking for a location for a new factory the local council was very helpful. A new industrial estate was being planned on the outskirts of Weston, called the Oldmixon Estate. One of the best corner sites had been allocated as a general car park but the council sold us half of it, which enabled us to build a small building of about 7000 square feet. A few years later, when we had expanded still more, we were to build an addition to this factory which doubled its area.

Eight months after the fire, in January 1971, our Oldmixon factory was ready, and at last we were able to have our offices, materials, dolls and sewing machines, as well as our manufacturing and painting areas all under one roof and on one floor. It was almost impossible to believe, and a great boost to our morale.

We spent days marking the floor with chalk, working from plans which we had been preparing for many weeks. The cutting machine, sewing machines, storage racks, desks and a reception area were all allocated their own spaces. We had never enjoyed such facilities before, as we had always been obliged to "make do." Now we were able to plan and organise a proper factory.

First and second Oldmixon factories, 1978.

Opening second Oldmixon factory by Sally Alford, T.V. Personality, June 1979. Left to right: Peggy Nisbet and Jack Wilson.

As far as was possible we tried to evolve a system whereby raw materials came in at one end of the factory and finished goods went out the other. It was not as simple as it sounds because of the multiplicity of stages and the complexity of making our particular dolls where there is so much handwork and detail. The one great problem was to avoid bottlenecks. Obviously, if, for example, there was a hold up at the machining stage, there would be no work the following week for the assemblers and finishers.

We also had to make provision for checking areas as we had six checks on dolls during their progress through the factory - 1) dolls upon arrival from moulders, (2) dolls after painting, (3) machined sets of clothes, (4) dressed dolls, (5) checks when ready for boxing and (6) final checks before box lids were put on ready for despatch.

By this time we were employing over 100 outworkers. They were composed of artists who painted the dolls, machinists who machined the sets of clothes, assemblers who hand-sewed the clothes onto the dolls and, finally, the finishers who added the accessories and put the wigs or styled the hair onto the models.

Sometimes we had a versatile outworker who would "make through" as we called it. Christine Westlake was one of these. She machined, dressed and finished *Mary Queen of Scots, Shakespeare, Pipers* and other characters, mostly men, for as mentioned previously, she is a trained tailoress.

There was one big mistake I made whilst the factory was being built. I was approached by a representative of a company selling "systems." Now I am not particularly system-minded, because I have found over the years that the energy and labour involved in setting up and carrying out these so-called "time-saving" schemes are so often less productive than an ordinary manual process. At least they were until computers came along.

However, I was persuaded that if we installed this ticket system we would know at any time of the day or night which outworkers had which batch of work. Strips were to be torn off the ticket indicating work issued, returned, paid for, etc., etc., etc. Not only did I install the system — and had a special glass see-through office built for it, but I engaged the salesman himself, supposedly an expert, to operate the scheme.

It was a new factory. I wanted it to run efficiently. I wanted to save my staff some of the drudgery of keeping records, writing out payment slips and, most of all, the physical stock-taking of dolls in production which we carried out each week.

The result? Disaster!!

It was immediately apparent that the system was not working. We had too many variables. However, we persevered and I hoped that by making adjustments it would succeed. Production and despatches were slowing down, rather than increasing, and we had innumerable complaints from outworkers whose work and payment slips were wrong.

A month or so after the installation of "The System," Alison and I had to attend a trade fair and were away for a week. We had left full instructions for the week's production and despatches.

On the Monday after our return, Syliva Bird showed me the previous week's figures, as was her usual practice. I looked at the despatch figures and was stunned. Instead of a despatch figure of several hundred, or even a thousand plus, there was one little solitary "6." We had a full order book, a new fully-staffed factory and over 100 outworkers, yet only six *Henry VIII* dolls had left the factory.

An immediate enquiry was started, as a result of which it became apparent that the system itself was not sufficiently flexible for the detailed nature of our work. No doubt with a skilled operator it could have been adapted to suit our method of manufacture, but the man we had engaged had obviously been incapable of processing the work. We could not afford the slowing down which would inevitably have taken place during the trial and error process, nor did we have the staff to do it. So it was abandoned, and to everyone's relief we carried on with our old procedures.

It took months to bring order out of chaos.

Apart from this error of judgment, the factory ran well and the company continued to expand, until we outgrew the new factory.

After the fire we had only built on half the land we had purchased because of our limited resources. Now we decided to build a two-storey extension.

In the meantime, we had become so cramped that it was decided to transfer the Design Department to my home at The Tower, where I had my study with all my reference books, and a spare room in which were installed my small design staff consisting of Mabel Perry (Design Assistant), a machinist (Mrs. Williams), driver (Muriel Turner) and last, but not least, Emily Wagstaff who not only looked after us and our meals, but prepared excellent luncheons for business guests, of whom we had many, and magnificent cold buffets for the groups of collectors from overseas and our own country who came to see the factory and have lunch with me afterwards. Some of these visits are described in another chapter. My son, daughter and myself always consider Emily Wagstaff to be one of the family. She came to me originally in 1965 after the sudden death of her husband, who was only in his forties. She was left with one newly married daughter, Joyce Wilmot, one daughter in her twenties, Margaret (now Margaret Pratt) and a young daughter, Susan, who was only four years old at the time of her father's death. She is now a midwife and lives in London with her husband, Tony Baden.

Emily Wagstaff lived near our Whitecross Road factory and, after her husband's death, she applied to us for a job. We employed her to clean our offices, but soon had other, more important things for her to do.

She is cheerful, capable and extraordinarily conscientious and loyal. Alison at this time had three babies under three years old, and was working hard with building the business. I also had my elderly Auntie Kitty, now in her eighties, and I did not want her left alone all day. Emily Wagstaff became indispensable, and has been so ever since. She looked after Alison's children and finally became my housekeeper, but retired in 1981 due to ill-health. Nevertheless, she still spends one day a week with me, and looks after my grandchildren on Sundays when Alison has her church duties.

Also working at The Tower, when I moved my staff into it, was Sue Worth, who has done all the artwork for this book. She remained on the staff until the sudden and unexpected death of her husband, after which she moved to Salisbury. Sue Worth is an accomplished artist with a flowing, open technique which appeals to me, and which in my opinion is eminently suitable for our character dolls. As Graphic Designer she has done all the artwork for this book. I particularly wanted The King of Arms, who proclaimed the Queen's Coronation, to appear to be proclaiming the publication of my book by introducing his picture on the front cover. This has, I think, been most effective.

Both Sue and I have tried to introduce a sense of heraldry throughout the book. She designed all the emblems and sketches which appear in our early letter headings, leaflets,

Oldmixon factory with Jerry Wiggin, Member of Parliament, examining Nisbet dolls.

73

catalogues and price lists, many of which are illustrated herein.

Sue recently sent me the following notes about herself and her family:

"After four years studying at Art School for a National Diploma in Design (Painting), I was apprenticed to a Conservator who specialised in the restoration of medieval monuments and effigies. These were located in Cathedrals, Churches and Country Houses (often in the care of The National Trust) so plenty of travel was involved. I often stayed in isolated and unusual places as well as familiar ones like Windsor, to work in the Queen's Chapel of St. George's, and Chatsworth, home of the Duke and Duchess of Devonshire. I even spent three weeks in an Elizabethan Manor House which was reputed to be haunted by Mary Fitton, a lady friend of William Shakespear and possibly his 'Dark Lady' of the Sonnets.

"Most of the monuments included the Coats of Arms of the family concerned so I became specially interested in the study of Heraldry. I was even fortunate enough to be offered special help in studying heraldic design and spent some very happy and rewarding hours in the studio of the resident designer at the College of Arms in London.

"I also needed to acquire some knowledge of historic costume as well as learning various specialised techniques like applying gold leaf in various ways.

"This essentially nomadic existence became impossible when I married an army officer only a year or so after I had gathered my own team of conservators. Not that an army life wasn't nomadic, but my husband, Joe, had served all through the war and travelled in a variety of ways. He even parachuted into Normandy the night before the Allied Landing in France. Our third child was born just after we eventually 'landed' in Weston-super-Mare. They are now all grown-up — having divided their student years at Oxford and Cambridge, two obtaining entry to Oxford and three to Cambridge.

"Although I had managed to fit in some freelance painting and drawing it was not until our fifth child was four years old and starting school that I first met Peggy Nisbet. She was, of course, well known to me by name and I had always admired her work. It was with some trepidation that I enquired about a part-time vacancy, hoping that my experience sewing my children's and my own clothes might be sufficient qualification.

"I soon found myself in her Design Department — as everyone else who works for Peggy, caught up by her enormous enthusiasm and search for perfec-

tion. The days went far too quickly — new projects, fresh ideas — Peggy has a wonderful ability to encourage and draw out any individual talent. She never made one feel one's ideas, however inexperienced, were not worth considering. My great sadness at having to move back to Salisbury when my husband died suddenly eleven years ago was certainly added to by leaving an employer whom I had come to regard as a personal friend.

"I have been delighted and honoured to be asked to work with her again on the production of this book."

In our design room, when a new model was completed, Mabel and I would make out a specification, which we inserted into a strong envelope together with patterns, clips of materials, sources of supply of materials, braids and trimmings with prices and delivery dates. Then our machinist, Mrs. Williams, would make five more sets of clothes, two of which Mabel dressed onto dolls. This meant that we now had three dressed dolls and three sets of clothes. One set of each we kept in the Design Department and two went to the factory: one to be kept as a reference and one to issue to the outworker.

Multiply this by dozens of new models introduced each year and the volume of work involved will be apparent.

Sadly, most of this, the most enthralling part of my own creative work, had to be done at nights and weekends, weekdays being totally occupied with production meetings, factory problems, bookkeepers, accountants, telephone calls, representatives from suppliers and daily problems of all kinds.

When the Oldmixon building was completed, Mabel Perry returned to the factory and became Design Assistant to Alison, thus providing a continuity of design.

The last range upon which Mabel Perry and I worked together included the models listed in our 1980 catalogue.

Upon listing the models in the Peggy Nisbet collectors' dolls range for inclusion in this book, there are approximately 800 items and I think some may be missing. I had personally designed and made the prototype of every single model with the assistance of Auntie Kitty and Mabel Perry. Not many people are aware of this fact, and I think it is important for collectors to know that every doll the company produced until 1980 was a genuine Peggy Nisbet model designed by me personally. It is a record of which I am proud, and which is probably unusual for a doll maker, many of whom employ other designers.

Later Jack Wilson moved the factory from the Oldmixon Industrial Estate in Weston-super-Mare to the village of Winscombe, eight miles away. He bought a small estate containing a Victorian building with outbuildings, used as the factory, alongside which is a lovely Victorian house and garden which is Jack and Alison's family home.

But that is another story.

Visits to U.S. Stores

——1975-1984——

Apart from the actual creation of dolls and the research involved, the most pleasurable times of my doll making years are when I am making doll tours in the U.S.A. and participating in the United Federation of Doll Clubs, Inc., conventions and the doll shows organised by leading stores.

It has been a great privilege to meet and talk with literally thousands of doll collectors, many of whom have become some of my greatest friends.

There is not sufficient space in this book to describe all these events but I will mention one or two of the most memorable doll shows and the unique experience of attending the annual U.F.D.C. convention.

During my 1975 tour in America I was a guest at Stewarts of Baltimore for a fortnight, taking part in a big British promotion to celebrate the American War of Independence.

This is the year when I started the Peggy Nisbet Doll Collectors' Club for which Sue Worth designed the membership card. The first membership cards were issued to my own family, immediately before my departure for the States and Baltimore collectors were given the first cards released to the public. The original card is here reproduced.

One of the highlights of my trip was a visit to Williamsburg. I had heard and read of all the restoration work which had been done and seen pictures of the historic buildings and the townspeople dressed in period costume; but one has to visit Williamsburg to wander in and out of the craft shops and along the roads and lanes, in order to appreciate the full beauty of the township and the feeling of history which pervades every nook and corner.

It was a wonderful experience and the inspiration which decided me to make, at a later date, the 1in (3cm) scale Williamsburg Collection.

Much of my time that year was spent in the Smithsonian Institution in Washington, D.C. I stayed for many hours in The Hall of The First Ladies, examining every detail of the original inaugural gowns, so that I could reproduce them as accurately as possible. Three of them were introduced in our 1975 range: *Martha Washington, Mary Lincoln* and *Jacqueline Kennedy.*

By far and away the most exciting and stimulating of all doll shows was the 1976 "Dolls in Revue" organised by Paul Starkey, toy buyer for the Daytons Hudson Department Stores. The doll show took place in Minneapolis. Paul has vision, enthusiasm, organising ability and an unsurpassed eye for detail. Moreover, he has a dedicated and loyal staff who support him totally. I had attended several interesting promotions of this kind in leading stores throughout the major cities in North America, all of them enjoyable and well presented, but Daytons "Dolls in Revue" was the first large scale event of its kind and was the forerunner of further spectacular shows

Peggy Nisbet Doll Collectors' Club Membership Card.

which were the envy of, and emulated by, toy departments throughout the world.

In Paul's words, "The original goal of the Doll Shows at Daytons was twofold:

1. To pull together as many of the world's best doll vendors into a show atmosphere so that our fine doll customers in Minneapolis could see and purchase these dolls.

2. To create a fun event that all people could enjoy whether they were serious doll collectors or not. We created a showplace for the fine doll clubs in our area to show and talk about their collections."

A press release entitled "A Gala Exhibit Spotlighting Daytons Dolls in Revue" states, "When Daytons Department Store, Minneapolis, opened its doors to a gala doll exhibition this September 16, it was not only children and collectors who rushed in. Daytons 'Dolls in Revue' combined contemporary with dated and antique dolls, and drew more than 12,000 visitors to their 12,000 square feet auditorium in its three day run. The actual attendance figures may be of interest: a remarkable achievement on Paul Starkey's part:

Peggy Nisbet and Paul Starkey at Daytons' "Dolls in Revue,"
Minneapolis, 1976.

Minneapolis, 1976. Daytons "Dolls in Revue."

Daytons 'Dolls in Revue' 1976:

Wednesday	September 15th	Evening Press Party	162
Thursday	September 16th	9:30 a.m. - 9 p.m.	2630
Friday	September 17th	9:30 a.m. - 5:45 p.m.	2521
Saturday	September 18th	9:30 a.m. - 5:45 p.m.	6872
			12185

Minneapolis, 1976. Daytons "Dolls in
Revue."

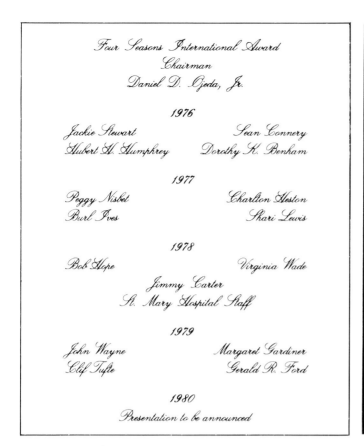

Four Seasons International Award
Chairman
Daniel D. Ojeda, Jr.

1976

Jackie Stewart   *Sean Connery*
Hubert H. Humphrey   *Dorothy K. Benham*

1977

Peggy Nisbet   *Charlton Heston*
Burl Ives   *Shari Lewis*

1978

Bob Hope   *Virginia Wade*
Jimmy Carter
St. Mary Hospital Staff

1979

John Wayne   *Margaret Gardiner*
Clif Tufte   *Gerald R. Ford*

1980
Presentation to be announced

Heritage Award Winners, Minneapolis, 1977.

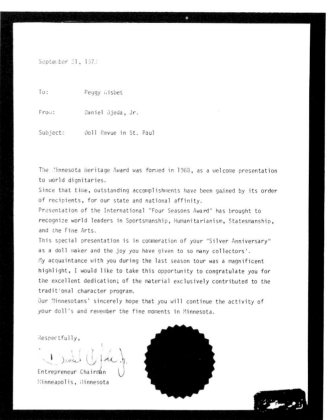

September 31, 1978

To: Peggy Nisbet

From: Daniel Ojeda, Jr.

Subject: Doll Revue in St. Paul

The Minnesota Heritage Award was formed in 1968, as a welcome presentation to world dignitaries.
Since that time, outstanding accomplishments have been gained by its order of recipients, for our state and national affinity.
Presentation of the International "Four Seasons Award" has brought to recognize world leaders in Sportsmanship, Humanitarianism, Statesmanship, and the Fine Arts.
This special presentation is in commemoration of your "Silver Anniversary" as a doll maker and the joy you have given to so many collectors'.
My acquaintance with you during the last season tour was a magnificent highlight, I would like to take this opportunity to congratulate you for the excellent dedication; of the material exclusively contributed to the traditional character program.
Our Minnesotans' sincerely hope that you will continue the activity of your doll's and remember the fine moments in Minnesota.

Respectfully,

Entrepreneur Chairman
Minneapolis, Minnesota

Heritage Award 1978, Minneapolis.

"Doll collecting fascinates millions, as attested to by the fact that it is the second most popular hobby in the United States after coins/stamps. Five area doll clubs lent their enthusiastic support, so both old and new worlds of dolls had the spotlight. From fifteen categories of collectable, dated dolls, the clubs chose their 'show offs': from 'French children' to 'German Bisque Girl Type' and 'American Ethnic'. The oldest doll was a Queen Anne wooden model from the 1770's, and in the middle spotlight of the collectable collections stood a wonderful dolls house dated from 1930, complete with every accessory a house of that period would have, including appropriately tiny patterned wallpaper."

The exhibit was organised by Edyth Casita. Paul Starkey arranged for her to visit the United Kingdom as a "thank you" for all her hard work and she came to stay with me for a few days.

Again I quote from another press release: "All these intricate, touchable and fragile collections posed challenges for display, security and lighting, the combination of which took several months of careful planning to resolve. The results were viewed on September 15 at on opening Press Invitation Party with raves. Based on pink coloured circles, painted on the auditorium floor, the exhibits were free standing and visible to every onlooker. Well-known British Doll Creator, Peggy Nisbet, explained the origins of her Costume and Portrait Dolls based on historical figures.

"Peggy Nisbet is perhaps best known and loved by doll fanciers, so Daytons held a special afternoon tea for her with doll club members. Mrs. Nisbet and the Doll Show also received enthusiastic publicity by the local media.

"Five Doll clubs from the Minnesota, Wisconsin area helped co-host this event:

1. Minnetonka Doll and Toy Club.
2. St. Paul Doll and Toy Club.
3. St. Croix Valley Doll and Toy Club.
4. Star of the North Doll Club.
5. Over the Rainbow Doll and Toy Club."

Some weeks later I received a letter from Paul Starkey, which I treasure. He said "We have just won First Award for Department Promotion from Playthings Magazine, and will be receiving this award at a dinner during the New York Toy Show.

"I cannot thank you enough for the important part you played in our show. We could not have asked for a better star to get our first show off the ground. I have talked to many of the Doll Club members since the show and they all have said how much they enjoyed meeting and talking with you."

The pleasure, of course, was mutual because I still have the happiest memories of the occasion. It was a fabulous experience which I shall never forget, nor, I am sure, will any of those who attended. I always looked forward to my annual Minneapolis visit more than to any other event and fortunately it was the only one which I attended every year, my itinerary varying from year to year in order to accept all the invitations extended to me. Paul Starkey always gave a superb dinner party for us all, and on the Sunday he would invite me to his home and take me with his family for trips on the lakes. Happy memories.

The story of "Dolls in Revue" cannot be completed without mention of some of the people who participated. In particular Paula Fox and Gladys Hall gave me so much support each year that I do not know what I should have done without them.

The Peggy Nisbet agents at that time were Reeves

Daytons Dolls, Minneapolis, 1986 — Elizabeth Tremble and Paula Fox.

Robert E. Moynihan, Reeves International, Inc.

Peggy Nisbet and Ted Cook (Reeves International, Inc.), Minneapolis.

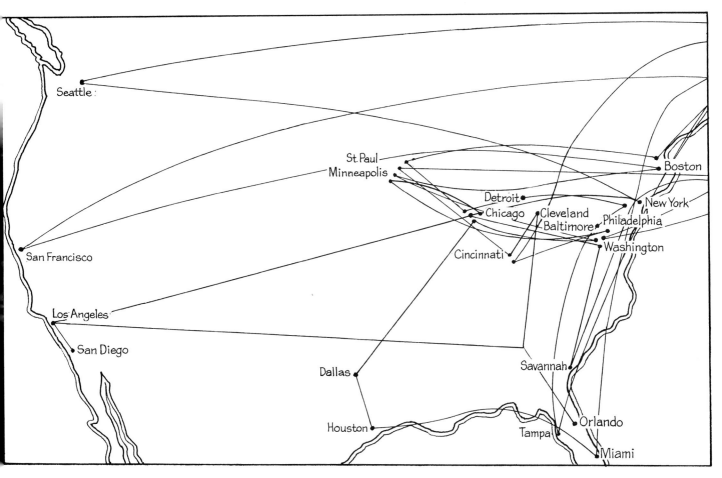

Map of visits to U.S. stores.

International, Inc., whose showrooms are at 1107 Broadway, New York, New York 10010. This is perhaps the time and place in which to pay tribute to Reeves for the excellent job they did for the company and for the magnificent support and the many kindnesses they showed to me personally. We were indeed fortunate in being represented by so efficient a firm of such high repute. The story of our association with them appears in Chapter XI, "Breaking into The Export Market," together with mention of Bob Moynihan and Ted Cook, who co-operated with Daytons in their promotions.

Very few of my readers will appreciate the difficulties of organising doll shows, tours and promotions, which are enjoyed by so many of the public, so it may be worthwhile digressing a little to describe some of the problems. As far as my own tours are concerned, the accompanying map will show the extent of some of my travels.

Most of the leading stores want to have their main promotions in September and October and they usually have a theme into which they gather some of their more interesting suppliers. Daytons happened to be a doll promotion, but others I have attended have included general as well as doll events. At a British promotion in Marshall Fields & Co. of Chicago, the store brought over from the United Kingdom The Lord Mayor of London himself and a Pearly King and Queen as well as some exquisite British historical costumes made by the famous costumiers, Berman and Nathan which were displayed on mannequins who paraded through the store at regular intervals; a Town Crier; Zara Rhodes, the dress designer and others whom I cannot remember. My

Design Assistant, Mabel Perry, accompanied me at this event and we were always surrounded by people who wanted to know about the characters' clothes and history. Marshall Fields had asked me to make a model of The Lord Mayor of London in his robes exclusively for them, so I went to the Mansion House in London. There I was invited in and shown the official robes which I copied meticulously. We only made a small number of these models, so there must be very few around in to-day's collections.

Other stores have an international theme, hand-crafts, food, general gifts and, of course, Christmas fairs. After Reeves had arranged a tour for me with the stores, Bob Moynihan attended to all the details, beginning with my arrival in the U.S.A. and ending with my departure for England. Normally I stayed for two months and spent one week in each store.

After booking my two airline tickets to and from America, Bob took over. He arranged internal flights and hotels and liaised continually with the stores involved. The stores, in their turn, organised press interviews, advertisements and articles in local papers, tea parties, breakfast parties for children and adults, whilst television appearances were arranged for me in every city I visited.

On one occasion the "To Tell the Truth" team tried to find me all over the U.S., and finally traced me to Washington, D.C. They asked me to participate in the programme, so instead of flying home as had been planned, I went to New York to record the programme. It was subsequently shown in New York, Los Angeles, Seattle, San Diego, Columbus, St.

Bob and Jean Hill.

Marshall Field & Co., centre-piece, Chicago, 1979.

Louis, Albany, Philadelphia, Tampa and Winston-Salem. Alas, they guessed who I was! It was an enjoyable experience.

An example of one of my tours is the one which included Daytons' "Dolls in Revue" described above. I arrived at Minneapolis on 6th September, spent a week at the Twin Cities, then went on to the following:

Shillito's, Cincinnati
Higbee's, Cleveland
Rich's, Atlanta
Bullock's, Los Angeles
Bullock's, San Diego
Woodward & Lothrop, Washington, D.C.

then to New York for the "To Tell the Truth" programme.

During this tour I met up with Dorothy Coleman, Bettyanne Twigg and Suzanne Gibson, all of whom collectors will know, and I went to New Jersey to see my old friends Bob and Jean Hill, who owned Wonderland Depot, Flemington, New Jersey, from whom so many collectors buy Peggy Nisbet dolls. I try to spend a few days with them and their family whenever I am in the U.S.A.

At Shillito's store in Cincinnati the assistants were so busy that one of our collectors, Eileen Halpern, who had come to buy dolls, ended up by acting as my sales assistant! She invited me to her beautiful home where she lives with her husband and two children. She kindly drove me to the airport when I left Cincinnati and still corresponds regularly. She and her daughter, Mimi, are dedicated collectors. They have been to visit me in Weston. Eileen is "trigger happy" when it comes to photographs and takes literally dozens at a time, some of

which she is good enough to send me for my album.

Amongst other stores I have visited are Jordan Marsh in Boston; Wannamaker's in Philadelphia; Nieman Marcus in Dallas and Houston; Stewart's in Baltimore; Macys in New York and San Francisco; Jacobsen's in Detroit and Frederick Nelson in Seattle.

In Seattle I spent a weekend with Bill and Martha Martin. Martha modelled, and Bill cast a doll to represent my granddaughter, Felicity, when she was a baby. They worked from a photograph I sent them. I always intended to make a range of baby dolls using this model but never got round to it, so the two photographed in this book are the only ones in existence, other than one head in glazed china which I keep in my home. Bill and Martha also organise tours and take groups to see collections in the United Kingdom and Europe. They are a delightful couple. I have included several photographs of Seattle doll collectors.

The few trips just described will illustrate a few of the friends I have made as a result of being a doll maker. It has been a wonderful experience to travel all over America and to meet so many different people. There are many anecdotes and reminiscences which come to mind as I am writing this book and which I should like to recount if I had the space.

Doll collecting is one of the friendliest of all hobbies: in fact, it is more a way of life than a hobby. It brings lonely people together and is far more educational than non-doll lovers appreciate, involving as it does history, architecture, furniture, clothes, different countries and environments and, most important of all — people.

Macys, New York, 1979.

Bill and Martha Martin.

Peggy Nisbet, Martha Kuehn,
Alison Wilson and Ken Kuehn,
Los Angeles, 1983.

Frederick and Nelson, Seattle,
1979.

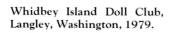

Whidbey Island Doll Club,
Langley, Washington, 1979.

Doll Collectors' Teaparty,
Seattle, September 1979.

Soft Toys,
Wooden Characters and
1 in (3cm) Scale Miniatures
———————1975———————

Just before Christmas in 1975 Roger Swinburne-Johnson, Chairman of The Chad Valley Co. Limited, telephoned me to say that it had been decided to close the Wellington factory where all their soft toys were made. He was very distressed at the dismissal of staff who had served him and his father before him for so many years, some of whom he had known since childhood.

Roger is a distant cousin of mine. We met regularly at toy fairs and it occurred to him that with our labour intensive production of handmade dolls, we might be interested in adding soft toys to our range and thus be able to take on some of his staff, particulary those skilled in the manufacture of jointed Teddy Bears.

Roger is a great-grandson of Anthony Bunn Johnson who started a printing and book-binding business in Birmingham at the end of the 18th century, which in 1897 became Johnson Bros. (Harborne) Limited with the registered trademark "Chad Valley" derived from the name of a little stream, The Chad, which flowed beside the new factory.

At the turn of the century the company started making simple toys, and in 1914 a range of Teddy Bears was added to the Chad Valley range. In 1920 the Teddy Bear production was moved to Wellington, Shropshire, and a new company, The Chad Valley Co. Limited was formed. This remained a family business until 1950 when it was declared a public company. Roger joined the company in 1935.

I told Jack and Alison of Roger's telephone call, and we arranged a meeting in Weston. After much discussion, we finally decided that it would be an interesting extension to our activities and a company was formed in 1976 called Nisbet Childhood Classics for the manufacture of high quality soft toys and Roger joined its Board as Managing Director.

In the first instance we took temporary premises in Telford, not far from the old Chad Valley factory and engaged some of their expert ex-staff. It proved to be impractical and uneconomic to have this unit so far away from our main factory, so we transferred the operation to Weston-super-Mare and retained the Telford staff as outworkers.

In addition to the original mohair Teddy Bears, we tried producing other soft toys, including dogs, cats and dressed bears.

About this time Marks & Spencer decided to introduce a

Roger Swinburne-Johnson and Peggy Nisbet.

small range of toys into their stores and approached us for samples.

Jack Wilson, Roger Swinburne-Johnson and I had several meetings at their headquarters in Baker Street, London, with the team who had been appointed to carry out the project.

We submitted a series of samples and finally an order was placed for a selection of models with which Marks & Spencer arranged to make test runs in some of the leading stores, as is their usual practice when trying out a new line. Several toy

Peggy Nisbet bears.

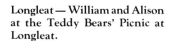

Longleat — William and Alison at the Teddy Bears' Picnic at Longleat.

firms, including Pedigree Dolls and other manufacturers of popular items, were also included in this project.

I do not think it was a complete success either for Marks & Spencer's or from our point of view. They had never sold toys before, so it was their first venture in this field. They delegated a team to the project and we spent a great deal of time with them developing the range. Our problem was the lack of experience of the Marks & Spencer team and their insistence on using materials which were totally unsuitable for the purpose. On one occasion they insisted on ordering

hundreds of yards of brown fur fabric with such a stiff backing that even the strongest needles broke in our sewing machines.

The Marks & Spencer team were enthusiastic and capable in a general sense, but they had no knowledge of soft toys. Each week a young member of the team came to Weston, swept into our factory and upset the machinists by telling them what they should and should not do when, of course, to follow her instructions would have been disastrous to the finished project. Members of my staff were placed in a very

Beatrix Potter characters, *Lady Mouse*, *Foxy Gentleman* and *Jemima Puddleduck*.

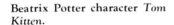

Beatrix Potter character *Tom Kitten*.

Peggy Nisbet and Muriel Turner visiting Beatrix Potter's Museum, 1979.

difficult position, not wishing to be discourteous and yet knowing that they could not follow these instructions.

Small test runs were made in one or two of the London stores which were apparently reasonable but not outstandingly successful. It was not a great surprise to me as far as our own product was concerned, because not sufficient time had been given to the development of the range and there were too many fingers in the pie: our own staff, the ex-Chad Valley staff and the Marks & Spencer team. If we had had a few months in which to consider the particular market and

develop specific models for it, it would have been very interesting and I would have enjoyed the challenge. I am a great fan of Marks & Spencer whose general efficiency is awe-inspiring and would have liked to have been associated with them. As it was, the whole toy project was abandoned by mutual consent.

Our second venture into soft toys was one after my own heart.

I had always been a great admirer of Beatrix Potter. Now that we were producing high quality jointed Teddy Bears I

Clown.

wondered if it would be possible to obtain the licence for the Beatrix Potter characters.

Tentative approaches were made to Frederick Warne & Co. Ltd., the publishers who hold all the Beatrix Potter rights. An appointment was made with their Chairman and Managing Director, Cyril Stephens, and I went to Frederick Warne's office in Bedford Square, London, and had a most interesting interview.

Cyril Stephens told us that soft toy manufacturers had been approaching Warne's for licences since 1909, without success. We showed him some of our traditional jointed bears and he was impressed with their quality. Finally he said that if we prepared samples which were acceptable to him, he would grant us the licence.

It was one of the most daunting tasks I had yet undertaken. Cyril Stephens was a perfectionist plus! Week after week Roger and I or Jack and I made trips to London. Cyril would say, "Yes, that is excellent, but ...." Then he would ask if we could bend a whisker here, or an ear there. The difficulty was that whereas we could make one prototype with one whisker at an angle of 45° and another at 75°, I could not guarantee that when we got into production we could comply with such accurate requirements because each of our needlewomen would work slightly differently. I had to tell him this but he was adamant that we had to accept his terms and stipulated that we should make two final prototypes for his approval. These had tags clamped onto them. One was retained by Warne's and one by ourselves.

We were granted the licence world-wide with the exception of the U.S.A. The New York offices of Frederick Warne had already granted a licence to a U.S. manufacturer for

10in (25cm) *Miss Muffet* **and** *Jack and Jill* **wooden peg tops, 1970s.**

North America only, so they could not give us this territory.

The pictures in this book, colour or black and white, do not show the character of the toys to advantage, nor the quality of the fur fabric we used. The most difficult to find was the cat material, with its long soft hair and tabby markings.

They were lovely models and I was so very proud of them. They were very unprofitable to make because of the high cost of both the material and labour. In addition to the full size models, we also made some dear little miniatures, which were quite enchanting.

Sadly, a few years ago my colleagues decided that it was uneconomic to continue to make the range. It was a sad moment. So much thought, care, time and trouble had gone into their development, and I was proud of them.

Previously we had developed another type of soft toy, entirely different from the Beatrix Potter range. This was a collection of modern silk screen printed characters.

Two groups were made under licence to the B.B.C. The first was from the children's programme "The Pogles of Pogle Wood," comprising Mr. & Mrs. Pogle, Pippin and Tog; the second was from "The Herbs," the characters being Sage, Dill and Parsley.

We tried to do the silk screen printing ourselves, but decided to give the work to a professional, and the fabric was printed for us by Amersham Prints Limited of Amersham, who did commissions for the John Lewis Partnership. Their work was perfect.

In addition to items under licence we designed and produced small pocket soft toys, a modern style rag doll and other characters which are illustrated herein. We also made 10in (25cm) wooden peg tops dressed as nursery rhyme characters and small 4in (10cm) dumpies. The latter was a souvenir range we introduced for W.H. Smith & Son airport Shops and Boots, the chemist stores.

In the silk screen medium we also produced, under licence, our best selling range of Dick Bruna characters, which are also illustrated in the colour section.

The story of our first order for these three models, *Miffy, Red Riding Hood* and *Eskimo*, is told in another chapter.

Dick Bruna was delightful to work with. On one occasion he held a reception at The Connaught Hotel, London. Dick sat beside me with a prototype of his characters, "Mary and Jesus" and "The Dwarf." He took out his pencil and re-drew a few lines, suggesting that I should make these small amendments. Shortly afterwards a fire destroyed our factory, as described elsewhere, and we were unable to proceed for the time being with any new models. However, I still have in my possession and cherish these two prototypes, which were never put into production. Fortunately, I had them at home with me at the time of the fire so they were not destroyed.

One project to which I was never able to devote enough time was the development of a "family" of 1in (3cm) to 1ft (31cm) scale dolls for dolls' house enthusiasts. So many collectors have asked me to do this.

When in the U.S.A. I attended many miniature functions and conventions. The intricacy and beauty of the work exhibited defies description.

In the 1970s we spent nearly two years developing a male and female miniature doll. I wanted them both to be fully articulated, so that they could stand and sit and be "real people" living in their small homes. The tooling was complicated and costly. I was too ambitious in my search for authenticity, and under-estimated the complexity of the task. The models were designed to move at the ankle, knee, hip, waist, shoulder, elbow, wrist and neck. I could have omitted some of these, e.g. wrist, ankle, and so forth, but alas, I did not do so. Not only was the tooling expensive, but the moulding and assembly were even more difficult.

Finally we introduced the "Victorian Collection" and the

Dick Bruna characters, *Red Riding Hood, Miffy* **and** *Eskimo,* **1970s.**

LEFT: 1in (3cm) scale miniatures, the Victorian Collection.

BELOW: 1in (3cm) scale miniatures, the Williamsburg Collection.

"Williamsburg Collection:" the latter intended to complement the beautiful Williamsburg miniature furniture I had seen during my visit there. Each collection consisted of a *Master of the House*; *Mistress of the House* (to demonstrate indoor clothes of the period); *Lady Visitor*; *Gentleman Visitor* (to demonstrate out-of-doors clothes of the period); *Maidservant* and *Manservant*. Later we introduced a set of *King Henry VIII and His Six Wives*, but it was the "families" in which I was most interested.

I designed a modern "Family Group" to live in 20th century dolls houses, but because of the complexity of the miniatures, my colleagues were not very enthusiastic about miniatures generally. Admittedly, they were difficult and not profitable. I always enjoy a challenge, but one must be practical when running a business, so I understand the reluctance to include them in our range.

I also intended having a little boy, little girl, and baby to complete the household. It is still one of my remaining ambitions to do this, and one day I will. I would welcome the views of miniaturists.

N/105 France (Riviera); N/110 Sweden; N/179 New Zealand; N/164 South America; N/139 Poland.

N/101 France - Brittany; N/146 Argentina; N/112 Spain; N/107 Switzerland; N/104 Italy; N/139 Poland.

Peggy Nisbet Dolls   *special collectors' edition*

P/1003 *Queen Nefertiti* of Egypt.

Design notes by Mrs. Peggy Nisbet.

Tutankhamen was a most interesting model to design. A great deal of research was necessary in order to produce an accurate representation of a pharoah who died over 3,000 years ago.

One of the greatest difficulties was to find the best manner in which to reproduce the famous head-dress, whilst at the same time retaining the white linen garments worn by nobles of that period.

Finally it was decided to model the head-dress, and mould it in gold metal painted to represent lapis lazuli, cornelian, quartz and turquoise. The magnificent collar, which would originally have been encrusted with lapis lazuli, cornelian, quartz, turquoise and feldspar has also been treated in the same way.

In his hands Tutankhamen carries a crook and a flail, the symbols of his title to the throne of the Sun God Osiris. His garment is made of white linen pleated in the form of a kilt, over which he wears the Royal Apron, also encrusted with lapis lazuli, turquoise and cornelian.

As soon as the prototype was completed it was taken to the Egyptology Department of the British Museum. An Egyptologist who examined it with his colleagues could find no fault, and their verdict was "It is very good indeed".

Certified and signed models of Tutankhamen will be offered as a limited edition of 1,000 dolls this year, after which unsigned models will be available from open stock.

During my tour of six American cities in the autumn of 1979 the limited edition of King Tutankhamen will be featured.

It is hoped that in 1980 we shall produce a model of the beautiful Queen Nefertiti. Tutankhamen and Nefertiti would make a spectacular pair for collectors.

Peggy Nisbet

King Tutankhamen

P1002 King Tutankhamen.

House of Nisbet Limited,
Oldmixon Crescent, Weston-super-Mare, England.

Harrods' Doorman (Special).

P/1009 *Peggy Nisbet* 30th Anniversary model.

P/796 Sir Winston Churchill
and P/822 Prime Minister
Margaret Thatcher.

P/615 Sir Winston Churchill and P/592 Lady Randolph Churchill.

P/630 Lord Darnley; P/608 Mary Queen of Scots (wedding); H/209 Mary Queen of Scots (Fotheringay).

BR/325 Black Watch Piper; H/224 Flora MacDonald; P/210 Charles Edward Stuart (Bonnie Prince Charlie).

P/719 Flora MacDonald.

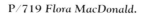

P/756 Stan Laurel; P/757 Oliver Hardy; P/754 Judy Garland; P/755 Charlie Chaplin.

P/705 Indian Warrior
(Bicentenary American
War of Independence);
H/817 British Redcoat;
H/816 American
Trooper.

A selection of catalogues.

Special set certificates from 1953
onwards.

Queen Elizabeth I: P/601 very early model; P/601 early model; P/601 early model.

Queen Elizabeth I - 8in (20cm) Peggy Nisbet bone china bisque with leather body.

Queen Victoria - 8in (20cm) Peggy Nisbet bone china bisque with leather body.

Full Circle -
Creation of Peggy Nisbet
Bone China Bisque Doll
—1976—

Ever since making my first china bisque doll in 1952 I had wanted to produce others in the same medium.

As explained in a previous chapter, it was originally impossible for practical and economic reasons to produce in china the large group of historical characters and souvenir costume dolls which it was my ambition to create, so the luxury of working in ceramics had to be forgotten.

In the early seventies, however, when my Silver Anniversary as a doll maker was approaching, I began to give serious thought to producing some of my favourite characters in bone china bisque. In order that my collectors could display the new range in their cabinets, it seemed necessary to keep approximately to the same size as my standard doll. On the other hand, I was anxious to have an extra inch or so to enable me to make the elaborate costumes in their stiff brocades hang properly. So I compromised and made them just over 8in (20cm) instead of our standard 7in (18cm) doll.

I would have preferred to make my own Peggy Nisbet china doll in our factory, but to open up a ceramic section was more than I felt I could undertake. Through an introduction I contacted Roger Turrell, who is Head of The School of Ceramic Design, Faculty of Art and Design, Bristol Polytechnic. It proved to be a wonderful partnership and Roger produced for us the ceramic heads, arms and feet for our well-known Tower Treasurers range, a photograph of which appears in my colour section.

Recently I spoke to Roger and told him about my book, asking him if he would describe his processes step by step. It seemed to me that collectors who are engaged in making their own dolls might be interested.

Also incorporated in the instructions is the formula or recipe which we finally adopted. Roger's subsequent letter to me reads:

"When I checked my records I was amazed to see that it was ten years ago that we first met to discuss the idea of making some trial ceramic dolls. To be more accurate, ceramic heads, arms and legs: as was the practice in dollmaking.

"The first trials were made using porcelain clay pressed into a plaster mould. This was a limited success - the surface was good but the colour was rather grey. Bone china was found to be better as it fired to a better flesh colour when ceramic stains had been added to the clay.

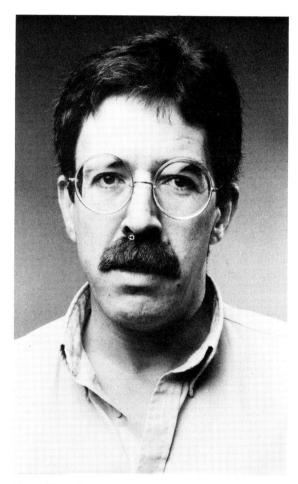

Roger Turrell.

"After many trials the following recipe was adopted:

Bone China	50%
China Clay	25%
Cornish Stone	25%

This is a standard bone china first made in England by Spode in 1794. A small quantity of bentonite (aprox 2%) is added to improve the working characteristics.

Arabella Stuart, **Peggy Nisbet bone china bisque, 1977.**

Queen Victoria, **Peggy Nisbet bone china bisque, 1976.**

Group of bone china bisque dolls, Tower Treasures, 1976-1978.

"A liquid preparation, called a slip, is then produced to the recipe:

Bone China Clay	50 kilos
Hot Water	5 litres
Sodium Silicate	175 mls
Stain	150 grms

Sodium silicate is a deflocculant, which is an agent for producing a fluid slip with the minimum water content. A proprietary ceramic stain - made from the metal oxides of iron, chrome and alumina - is added to the slip to produce the flesh colour.

"This slip is now passed through a 120 mesh sieve to make sure of complete mixing of all the ingredeints.

"After standing for a few days the slip is poured into plaster moulds, made from the original model. The excess liquid is drained from the moulds after 1-2 minutes, depending upon the thickness required. The moulds are left for approximately one hour for the cast to dry and harden, and then the piece is carefully removed. After drying the seam marks are cleaned off and any necessary holes are made. Great care is needed at this stage as the unfired piece is extremely delicate.

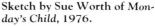

Sketch by Sue Worth of Monday's Child, 1976.

"When completely dry, after 24 hours, the cast pieces are placed on kiln shelves in a layer of alumina hydrate and packed into the kiln. A 12 kilowatt Bricesco TL27 kiln was used for all firings. After 15-16 hours the kiln temperature is 1250° C, and the firing is complete. The control of the temperature is crucial as the bone china clay can distort very easily producing bizarre results.

"The dolls produced were:

1976	*Queen Elizabeth I*	
	Queen Victoria	
1977	*Queen Elizabeth II*	
	Herald	(full figure)
	Arabella Stuart	
	Prince Philip	(full figure)
1978	*Lady Jane Grey*	
	Queen Elizabeth II	(Coronation)
	Princess Elizabeth	
	Princess Margaret	
	Queen Mary Tudor	
	Mary, Queen of Scots"	

The Silver Jubilee of the accession of Queen Elizabeth II to the throne would be taking place in 1977, and it seemed appropriate that a Peggy Nisbet doll should be designed to commemorate the occasion and to complement my first china bisque coronation doll. It would, I knew, take at least two years of research, but there was just time to do it. What fascinating work it was, and what an enormous amount of help I received from everyone, including officials at the Tower of London and various government departments. In Chapter 24 there appears the story of my efforts.

In order that there should be no confusion between our standard dolls and the new china bisque models, it was decided to sell the new bisque range direct to collectors through the Peggy Nisbet Doll Collectors' Club.

There is no doubt about it: I am a glutton for punishment! As soon as I have surmounted one difficulty, I seem to have a compulsion to try and create something else, and thus give myself further problems.

The 8in (20cm) china range had proved a success. Now my thoughts turned to a larger doll.

This would be quite beyond Roger Turrell's capacity with the limited equipment and time at his disposal. The Staffordshire Potteries would appear to be the answer, but upon making enquiries I found that no dolls had been made by any factory for years and so it meant breaking new ground.

Amongst others approached was a small company called Healacraft, whose work I had admired. The Healacraft factory was compact, well organized with a staff of experienced Staffordshire potters whose families had worked in the industry for generations.

The Managing Director was Alan Taylor, whose wife, Betty, was the Company Secretary.

When I first approached them, Healacraft was engaged in the manufacture of bowls of flowers and similar gift items in fine bone china. The quality of their ware was excellent and I asked Alan if he would be interested in making china heads, arms and legs for us.

The factory, in common with other Staffordshire Potters, had no experience of doll making but Alan was interested and

Signing of agreement, Royal Doulton/Nisbet, November 1980.

spent a considerable amount of time in experimental work.

I was anxious to have a theme for this new venture and having discussed it with my colleagues, it was agreed that we should make a series of seven dolls representing the Seven Days of the Week. Thus was born "The Days of The Week" series.

In order to obtain characterization, I turned out all my boxes of old family photographs, and asked Sue Worth if she would sketch some of them from which the modeller could work. My sister, children, grandchildren and myself became the "models." Sue did some quick drawings and one of the sketches is reproduced in this book. It is a very rough sketch, all of them having been done in an hour or so sitting on the floor at her home. Sue does not think they are good enough to reproduced but my own view is that collectors like to know how ideas start and develop into a finished article.

Whilst the modelling was being done, Alan continued with his experiments and finally decided on the following formula:

     50% Animal bone
     25% China clay from Cornwall China Clay Pits
     25% China stone

Alan then developed a matt glaze after many experiments to achieve the best skin texture. He fired at 1300° C. There were three firings.

Almost immediately after designing the clothes and seeing first prototypes, I left for my tour of the U.S. stores, a trip which I made annually. During my absence Jack and Alison continued with the development of the project and decided that the range should comprise fourteen models instead of seven. I had made provision for five girls and two boys, but Jack and Alison thought that there should be seven

boys and seven girls so that there was one of each sex for every day of the week. Consequently, on my return from my U.S. trip I found the models in the "Days of The Week" series had increased from seven to fourteen. Jack had also worked out a schedule, which he printed. This showed at a glance the day of the week appropriate to the date of birth and it proved to be a great attraction because so few people remember the day on which they are born. Now all they had to do was refer to the schedule.

Not long after Healacraft had started making the doll parts, and were running them through the factory satisfactorily, disaster struck them. The china factory was flourishing, but the holding company got into financial difficulties. The factory was closed and production ceased.

It was at this point that Jack became more interested in china dolls than he had been in the initial stages. Healacraft dolls had whetted his appetite and he wanted to continue with china models. Once Jack takes on a project, he works at it day and night with undiminished enthusiasm. He decided to approach one of the leading manufacturers of china figurines who would have the necessary techniques and contacted Royal Doulton. He suggested to them that their skills as potters, combined with our skills with dolls' costumes, would make an excellent combination, and so it proved to be. Thus was born the Nisbet Doulton range of fine bone china dolls.

A joint Nisbet/Doulton reception was held at The Savoy Hotel in 1981 to launch the project. Dorothy Coleman and her daughter, Jane, were flown over to London. Guests included Faith Eaton, Gwen White, Caroline Goodfellow, Mary Hillier, Betty Cadbury and many other British doll collectors. They all brought their favourite dolls with them.

100

Nisbet/Royal Doulton meeting: Alison Wilson, Jane Coleman, Peggy Nisbet, Dorothy Coleman and Keith Pybus (Doultons).

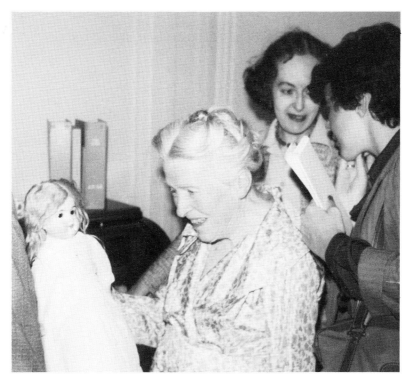

Gwen White and Faith Eaton at Nisbet/Doulton Reception, Savoy Hotel, London, 1981.

Dorothy Coleman, Caroline Goodfellow and Mary Hillier at Nisbet/Doulton Reception, Savoy Hotel, London, 1981.

Mary Hillier, Betty Cabury, Dorothy Coleman at Nisbet/Doulton reception, Savoy Hotel, London, 1981.

The Creation of a New Model

The one question that every collector asks me is how do I select the models I want to create and having selected them, how do I turn the dream into a reality.

The most exciting and rewarding part of building the business has been deciding upon a new character and then, having made the decision, collecting around me books and articles of all descriptions so that I know as much as possible of the character, background, history and clothes of my subject. There is, alas, never enough time to do as much as I would like.

Most of my research is done in libraries and museums but I have a magpie mind and love collecting scraps of information so whenever I travel, I carry with me a pen, notebook and a pair of scissors. I buy books, magazines and newspapers; then I go through them with great enjoyment, cutting out anything and everything that is even remotely connected with my work, making voluminous notes of any facts which seem to be relevant.

Doll collectors enjoy their hobby and I believe do not necessarily want an exclusively academic approach, so they will understand this light-hearted account of my quest for authenticity. On the more serious side, I obtain much of the characterization itself from the National Portrait Gallery in London where I have spent many hours sitting and looking at a portrait and noting every detail of costume. I leave the gallery armed with any books, postcards and posters which portray the character I have been studying and sometimes go on to the British Museum or the Victoria and Albert Museum.

The next stage is to go to my own personal library of costume books and study the clothes of the period. If I feel I need still more information I go to the local Public Library at Weston-super-mare where. If the librarian does not possess the book I require, he will willingly obtain it from another part of the country.

I have been very lucky in this respect. Weston has had two of the ablest and most dedicated of librarians, Geoffrey Rye, F.L.A. (Fellow of Library Association) and John Loosley, A.L.A. (Associate of Library Association).

When I first started researching costumes and historical characters, it was Geoffrey Rye who went to enormous trouble to answer my queries. He was the librarian at Weston from 1951 to 1974, so had to bear the brunt of most of the questions in the very early days. He reminded me of an occasion when I had been asked by a government department to produce 24 dolls representing different countries in their authentic national costumes. These were required as gifts for an important banquet being given to visiting dignitaries from overseas and were to be placed on the table, one before each lady guest.

When designing my model of Flora MacDonald, I wanted to use the MacDonald tartan, but our research indicated that Scottish ladies of quality did not at that time wear tartan dresses. So Geoffrey took the trouble to get in touch with Mr. Minter, Chief Librarian in Edinburgh, who spent some time on the problem. He must have found the portrait of Flora by Sir Alan Ramsay, where she wore a tartan dress with a white mob cap, because this is the picture I used as a guide.

Geoffrey was kind enough to say that I was able to do a little in return for all the help he gave me, because when making his reports to the powers that be, he was able to say that his library was not only there to lend books for leisure reading, but it was also of help to industry in that it helped small companies like ours, who were without the resources to undertake expensive and sophisticated research to "get off the ground," as he put it.

Geoffrey Rye and his wife are keen English folk dancing enthusiasts. They once took a dancing team to Sweden and I made a model of one of the local Morris Dancers which they presented to the King of Sweden.

My first encounter with John Loosley, Geoffrey Rye's successor was a surprising one. It was an enquiry connected with our company and I cannot even remember the subject but I knew there had been an article about it in the local press, so I asked John if they had any record in the library of the event. He said "Oh, yes, of course we have. There is a complete file here on the history of your company." It did not seem possible to me that we should be of sufficient importance to warrant a file amongst the local archives. But there it was, bulging with notes, photos and newspaper cuttings and I have even had to refer to it from time to time during the writing of this book.

John says, "Since the start of the Peggy Nisbet doll business, the library in Weston-super-Mare has been involved in finding an incredible amount of detailed information about the dresses of a wide range of historical and contemporary figures."

John Loosley, A.L.A., Area Librarian, Woodspring Central Library, was born in Luton, Bedfordshire. In 1974 he was appointed librarian for the Woodspring area in the County of Avon Library Service based in Weston-super-Mare, the post he holds today.

After having researched my subject thoroughly, my next task is the modelling. This has to be done at an early stage because the process of making the moulds is such a lengthy one and there is so much trial and error. It is difficult to capture the likeness of some characters, particularly those whose faces rely on their expression, without which their features fade into anonymity.

Modern dress is not easy on so small a scale; by far the

Mabel Perry arranging display of dolls to commemorate the Investiture of Prince of Wales at Caernarvon Castle, 1969.

most difficult being the group of the royal family which I designed to commemorate the Investiture of The Prince of Wales at Caernarvon Castle in 1969.

It was the year of miniskirts, even hemlines of The Queen's dress fell only just to the knee. It was a nightmare getting the proportions right on so small a figure, the dresses being straight, short and tight, so that from shoulder to hem they were only a few inches.

Medieval, Tudor, Elizabethan and Georgian costumes were my joy, when I could indulge my love for fabric designs, colours and textures.

I am by nature a perfectionist but when creating my dolls, I rarely attain the perfection for which I aim. The very fact that I must be able to supply all my customers with the dolls they require means that I have to be practical as well as theoretical. For example, many of the fabrics used in the past are no longer

available nor is it possible, leave alone practical, to obtain them. For real whalebone we now have to use a nylon substitute and, although we can still obtain cambric, cottons, brocades, taffetas, silks and satins, many of these are now composed of man-made fibres, so they look and hang differently from their original fabrics.

Again, having found the nearest weight and texture of cloth, we still have to find designs which are in proportion to our 7 to 8in (18 to 20cm) collectors' doll. Fortunately, over the years I have established connections with mills throughout the U.K., so I am frequently able to obtain designs woven specially for us. For example, we have 100% wool authentic tartans woven for us in miniature in Scotland, brocades woven to our design in England and traditional flannels woven for us in Wales.

I follow no golden rule when deciding to make a new

Peggy Nisbet with General Election Models of Prime Minister Margaret Thatcher, 1979.

Peggy Nisbet in artroom with Karen Phipps and Sylvia Hooper.

model. My mind is always seething with ideas for characters that I want to create and I have rows of files called "Development" which get fatter and fatter as I jot down ideas and add pictures and articles of one kind or another. There is enough information for many years of work and it is frustrating not to be able to do them, for collectors to add them to their collections.

In the past, some of my problems were solved when collectors wrote and asked for a particular character and when I speak at conventions, or attend doll functions, I am inundated with requests for characters which various collectors would like to buy to complete a particular collection or project they have in hand. If the subject is likely to be of general interest, I add it to my list of suggested new models. On many occasions it is a doll I have already wanted to do, so if it is one that I know collectors require, I start researching it.

Now comes the part that I enjoy most of all. First I research the subject and the period, then the costumes, then the materials and colours.

This is the point at which I emerge from my study and go

into Mrs. Perry's little sanctum. We sit together and plan the whole costume after which patterns are cut and the model is under way. Sometimes everything goes smoothly; at other times patterns are cut and re-cut, adjusted and re-adjusted, until at last we are satisfied with the result.

Before Mabel Perry joined the company, Auntie Kitty worked with me on every model, and together we made the first prototype. She cut out each pattern as we went along, whilst I tried pinning different materials and colours together until I achieved the costume I had in mind. We discarded most of the patterns, whilst we re-arranged and adjusted them, but it was the only way I could keep a record, step by step, of what we were doing. Mabel worked closely with Auntie Kitty, until the latter's arthritis prevented her from doing the detailed work. She passed on her knowledge to Mabel who, from then onwards, worked with me on the prototype of every new Peggy Nisbet model.

An ordinary dress designer could do a sketch and work from it, with some idea of what the result would be, having certain guidelines already established, but with our tiny models and my limited experience in the beginning with working on so small a scale, it was very difficult to envisage the way in which the folds would fall, particularly as most materials were too heavy and stiff. A fraction of an inch added to, or taken off from a bodice or sleeve would alter the appearance entirely. Even a tiny bit too much taken in at the seam would make a bodice ill-fitting. This latter point was one of our greatest difficulties in production when we were using outworkers. A needlewoman would bring back an ill-fitting garment, having used our pattern and done an excellent bit of machining but having taken in just a little too much or too little in the seam.

I am sure that trained dress designers would be horrified at my methods, but then I am not a trained dress designer, so I just had to work in my own way. My aim was to make each model as accurate and well-made a reproduction of a period costume as possible and to capture the character of the subject and the period with as much authenticity as was practicable.

In the very early days Jean Hancock, of whom I have written elsewhere in this book, cut out and machined a few of the patterns of the 6in (15cm) *Happy Doll* series. Mabel Perry and I have a rapport which I greatly miss now that I am no longer working with her, but she and Alison are carrying on the good work and liaising well together.

Collage showing processes of dressing a doll.

Sue Worth.

106

The Production Of A Catalogue

Every year we had to produce a new catalogue. Twelve months before this was due I started my planning. This was when I would get out all my development files, spread them all over the floor, and begin digging into their contents. There would already be lists of "musts" to which I had added throughout previous months, but these always exceeded the number of new models which could be introduced.

Collectors want more and more new models from which to choose and I would willingly create more and more new characters, but one has to be practical, so each year we tried to delete from our range as many dolls as we introduced. For many years I created an increasing number of new characters. At the beginning my range was so small and our business was growing so rapidly, that we needed the additional items, but as the list became larger, production and economic problems arose. Shops did not want to wait for deliveries, which meant that if we gave them good service we had to keep stocks of all our models. This meant tying up money in our stock which we needed for running the business. Each year our Chairman, backed by our accountants, said the same thing: "Your stock figure is too high!" In 1972 we had so many dolls in our range that we had to cut down drastically, and from thence forward only put in the same number as we took out.

My selection of new models would normally start at least one year before they were due to be introduced. The exceptions were Jubilee year and U.S. Bicentennial models, upon both of which I worked for two to three years before the dolls were put on the market.

Normally my Christmas and New Year treat to myself was, once the family festivities were over, to sit in my study and make my first list of dolls I wanted to introduce 12 months hence. The factory was closed for the holiday and there was a wonderful uninterrupted period of time when I could think and plan and prepare an itinerary.

By the time the factory re-opened after the holiday, my first list was ready. It was a long one, and would be shortened and then shortened again for practical reasons.

First of all I asterisked the "musts" and I immediately started research into the characters and costumes. Visits to museums, places of historical interest and libraries continued throughout the winter, together with sessions with modellers and manufacturers of fabrics, ribbons, braids, diamante and the hundred and one accessories required.

Immediately after the toy fairs, and still early in the year, we had our first meeting to discuss progress. I produced some of the "musts," in a partly completed form, together with rough mock-ups of other models on my list. These were discussed and a date fixed for an Easter meeting, by which time more dolls would be ready for discussion.

At Easter I made a short list and the bulk of new models was decided upon. This could not be left any longer because when new modelling and new moulds were required, the time element was beginning to be tight. Instructions were given to the modellers, and the range began to take shape.

By June I had a final short list ready, with all the models set before us on a table in various stages of completion. This was THE important meeting because the next one would be the photographic session in August or early September when every model had to be ready for the camera.

Photography usually took two days, during which no telephone calls were allowed to disturb us. Mabel Perry was always in attendance with needle, thread, scissors and the all-important dressmaker's pad of pins, so that skirts could be lifted or dropped to make a better picture. The sessions were normally in the factory or The Tower, but on one occasion we went to the photographer's studio in Chelsea, London: a vast high barn-size room with sophisticated cameras, equipment and lighting swinging overhead as in a television studio.

Once the film had been processed, lists and prices were assembled, and the following year's catalogue sent to the printers. Copies had to be in the hands of our overseas agents by November, so that they could be incorporated into their own catalogues and, of course, supplies had to be ready for our domestic trade fairs, the first of which was the gift fair at Torquay in early January. Then followed the International B.T.H.A. Toy Fair, originally held in Brighton, then Birmingham and now London; The International Gift Fair originally in Blackpool and now in Birmingham; the Nurnberg Toy Fair in Germany and the American International Toy Fair in New York City. These were the main fairs that we attended.

After Jack joined us, our price lists, catalogues and advertising literature became much more sophisticated. With his Letraset training behind him, he was an expert on modern calligraphy and marketing procedures. He was very much interested in this side of the business and became totally involved and responsible for it.

The photographs for the colour transparencies and black and white prints for this book were taken by Graham Wiltshire and Cliff Atyeo of Orchard Studios, Weston-super-Mare. In my opinion they are the best set of photographs we have ever had taken, and the two photographers should be congratulated on doing a superb job.

Peggy Nisbet

Peggy Nisbet Ltd. trade price list, 1971.

Peggy Nisbet Ltd. catalogue, 1960s.

TOWER TREASURES
TRADE PRICE LIST

2½" DUMPIES

DANCES OF THE WORLD		each
F/1	Tarantelle (Italy and Sicily)	12/-
F/2	Mazurka (Poland)	12/-
F/3	Flamenco (Spain)	12/-
F/4	Ländler (Austrian Tyrol)	12/-
F/5	Gavotte (France)	12/-
F/6	English Folk Dancing—girl	
F/7	English Folk Dancing—Morris Man, North West England	12/-
F/8	Royal Scottish Country Dancing, Girl	12/-
F/9	Royal Scottish Country Dancing, Man	12/-
F/10	Irish Jig—Girl	12/-
F/11	Irish Jig—Man	12/-
F/12	Welsh Country Dancing—Girl	12/-

• these items have won an award in the Council of Industrial Design / British Travel Association Competition for British Souvenirs.

D/1	• England (London)	
D/2	England (Country Maid)	
D/3	Scotland (Piper)	
D/4	Scotland (Highland Chieftain)	
D/5	• Ireland (Colleen)	
D/6	• Wales (Traditional)	

Price per carton of six assorted (one of each kind) in individual display packs 33/-

Any one of the models may be ordered in cartons of six 33/-

As the Dumpy Range has been designed specially for the Souvenir and Tourist Trade, we are prepared to design and make special models of local interest

BRITISH UNIFORMS		each
K/1	Guardsman	12/-
K/2	Beefeater	12/-
K/3	Lifeguards	12/-
K/4	Scots Piper	12/-
K/5	Gentleman at Arms	12/-
K/6	Policeman	12/-

4" DUMPIES

D/7	Guardsman	
D/8	Piper	

Price per carton of six of one kind in individual display packs 33/-

Tower Treasures trade prist list, 1960s (page 1).

7½" BRITISH UNIFORM RANGE

Tower Treasures illustrations (pages 2 and 3 spread).

108

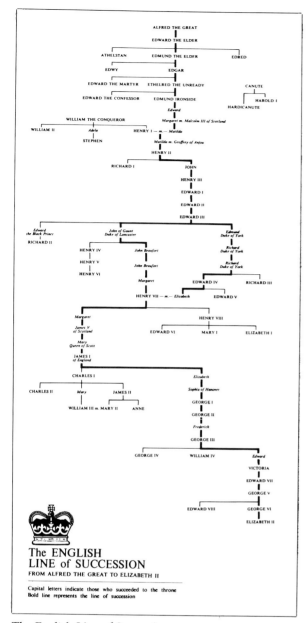

The English Line of Succession.

Peggy Nisbet Ltd. price lists and catalogues, 1953-1978.

A ROYAL WEDDING

H.R.H. Prince Charles, The Prince of Wales
Lady Diana Spencer, St. Paul's Cathedral
29th July, 1981

The announcement of the Royal engagement ended
of intense speculation over the most publicised
ever conducted by a future British Monarch.
most momentous piece of Royal news since th
Coronation twenty-seven years ago.

Prince Charles was born on 14th November, 1948
Diana Spencer on 1st July 1961. They are b
descendants of the Tudor King, Henry VII.
are, in fact, 16th cousins once removed. Whe
becomes King he will be Britain's 64th Sovereign.

The wedding was a nationwide celebration, wait
watched by satellite television all around the wor
place on 29th July, 1981, at St. Paul's Cathe
Cathedral was chosen because St. Paul's will
3,000 people, hundreds more than Westmins
The last Prince of Wales to be married at St.
Henry VIII's elder brother, Arthur Tudor.
1501 in the old St. Paul's which was destroyed i
Fire of London in 1666. This is the first time fo
three hundred years that the Heir to the throne
has married a British subject. In 1659 Charles
James (later James II) married Lady Anne Hyde
the first time for sixty years that Britain has ha
of Wales. The wedding was conducted by the
of Canterbury, Dr. Runcie.

Royal Wedding Commemorative Set
Special Collectors' Set No. 19
CERTIFICATE

*We hereby certify that those Peggy Nisbet dolls of
H.R.H. Prince Charles, The Prince of Wales,
model P1004 and H.R.H. The Princess of Wales,
model P1005 comprise:*

SET NO. ....

of a Signed Limited Edition of 4,000 Sets.

*We guarantee that no further signed Royal Wedding
Commemorative Sets will be made.*

Peggy Nisbet, *Founder*

Alison Nisbet, *Design Director*

John S. Wilson, *Chairman*

House of Nisbet Ltd., Dunster Park, Winscombe BS25 1AG England

... Dolls by House of Nisbet Ltd.
...bject to substitution, These are original Peggy
...ich artistic copyright is claimed. Any instance
...ght to our notice will be prosecuted.

Hand made in England

"A Royal Wedding" certificate.

Specials

The models that I have designed exclusively for stores, hotels, airlines and other customers are so numerous and varied that they cannot be described fully in this book, where the space available is so limited. Mention must be made of some of them, however, but the reference to them must of necessity be brief.

In the Peggy Nisbet Collectors' Dolls ranges I was asked to do many exciting and varied dolls, as exclusive items.

Some of the leading stores have asked us to make models exclusively for them. My first bisque doll was, of course, made exclusively for Harrods. Thereafter we made others for them, the most popular of which was probably the well-known figure of Harrods' doorman. How many thousands, nay millions of their customers have queued up for a taxi, and been solicitously and courteously ushered into one by the beneficent figure, at whose signal every taxi driver in London will come hastening to his bid. How well he controls his queue of parcel-laden, tired but satisfied customers, staggering under the weight of their purchases.

Bob Marchant, the Toy Buyer at Harrods, first approached me in the early seventies and suggested that I should design a doorman for them. We went to a considerable amount of trouble to get the correct colour and weight of cloth, which was our main problem. We decided that it had to be a very expensive "face cloth" which is normally used for top quality suits, and is particularly soft and supple. I made the prototype which Bob Marchant approved, but I did not at once put this into production. I do not remember why I dragged my feet over this one: it might have been as a result of the fire when I tried to keep to absolute necessitities, but the prototype remained on Mabel Perry's shelf for some time.

When Jack and Alison started to run the factory, Harrods' doorman came to life and was included in their range. It has proved to be a most popular model. Harrods themselves designed the box, which is perfect for showing the model to full advantange. An illustration appears elsewhere.

For Hamleys we have produced an exclusive model or models every year for inclusion in their catalogue. Peggy Lines, the daughter of Walter Lines who created the vast Lines Brothers toy empire, asked me to design some special characters for the Queen's Silver Jubilee. Peggy Lines was at that time Managing Director and very involved in the doll section. I made special models of The Lord Chamberlain, The Lord Chief Justice, The Earl Marshall and The Royal Herald. (See color section.)

Other exclusive models we have done for Hamleys include a *Regency Lady* and *Regency Gentleman*. The following year we introduced the *Regency Grandmother*, using a delightful Liberty cotton print so very suitable for the costume. They all sold well.

Peggy Lines also asked me to do some finger puppets. These I made in felt and the range included a guardsman, piper and a few others I cannot now remember.

Hamleys is still one of the most famous toy shops in the world but it has had some dramatic changes of ownership over the last few years. Brian Griffin has been outstanding in the way he has maintained the quality and variety of toys in this great British institution. Doll collectors should be grateful to him for his knowledge of their requirements. Brian is, at the time of writing this book, the Managing Director of Hamleys. There are rumours of another change in the ownership of the store so I do not know what the future will hold.

Nisbet dolls inspired by the characters from the film "Oliver."

I cannot leave my story of Hamleys without mentioning Miss Locke who was the Hamleys' buyer for so many years. She retired recently but will always be remembered for her contribution to the world of doll collecting.

When Miss Locke retired, the Chairman gave a luncheon party in her honour to which I had the privilege of being invited, and which all the leading British toy manufacturers attended. Miss Locke was dedicated to Hamleys and to her dolls, and had an instinct which seemed to tell her what her customers required.

When Alison and I went on the Jetsell mission, which is described in another chapter, we started negotiations for the production of a range of dolls to be made exclusively for BOAC (British Overseas Airways Corporation), now British Airways.

This was primarily Alison's project, although we were both involved. Alison developed and brought negotiations to a conclusion, and the result was an order for 17,000 dolls. BOAC selected 17 characters including a pilot, steward, air hostess and a range of British characters such as policemen, guardsmen, Welsh girls, Scottish dancers, and so forth. We had to make 1000 each of the 17 characters, deliveries to be made on agreed dates. These dolls were illustrated in their magazine which was distributed in every plane they flew, from which they operated a mail order service.

At a later date BEA (British European Airways) asked us to design and supply an exclusive range for them. These were mainly national costumes of various countries.

Other "specials" we made which were connected with transport by air and sea were the well-known *Sailor Boy*, originally made by Norah Welling and produced for the Cunard Line, but also supplied to the P. & O. line and other shipping lines. They are now treasured collectors' items.

We made a group of *Belly Dancers* - all sequins and glamour - for a convention taking place here in the U.K. but ordered by one of the Arab states.

One large group of hotels ordered a specially designed doll every Christmas as a gift for their lady guests on Christmas Day.

For Canada we made a number of exclusive models, including a "Mountie" (Royal Canadian Mounted Police) and a dancing girl wearing a kilt in the Nova Scotia tartan. There were many other special Canadian models.

Cadbury's asked us to make them some models to advertise their Elizabethan chocolate wafers. This was for a self-liquidating promotion which was well advertised nationally and Cadbury's were an excellent company with whom to work.

The list is endless.

Some of the above are not numbered in the pages of models listed in this book, as many of them were never given numbers because they were not for general sale. We have no records other than from my memory.

This chapter cannot be concluded without mentioning three sets of specials in which I was particularly interested - in each case illustrations are included in this book.

In 1968 Dr. David Milner wrote to me from The Department of Psychology at The University of Bristol. He was doing some research in connection with coloured immigrant children, and asked if I could help by letting him have three boy and three girl dolls, each group to comprise one each of a white child, brown child and black child. He asked if we could dress each group in simple identical costumes.

Belly Dancer.

Doll of Peggy Nisbet to commemorate 30th Anniversary of the foundation of the business (1953-1983).

Although this sounds a simple undertaking, Mabel Perry and I spent many hours selecting, colouring and painting the dolls, then dressing them afterwards.

Three years later I received a letter from Dr. Milner saying that his research was completed. He sent me a copy of an article he had written on the subject in the current issue of *New Society*. He further stated that this research was extremely successful and was to be the subject of a book he was writing for Penguin Books. He was kind enough to say that the dolls greatly contributed to the success of the research.

This project gave me a tremendous amount of pleasure. It proved my frequently expressed opinion, which I know is held by Dorothy Coleman, Faith Eaton and many others, that dolls play a great part in the social history of a country or civilization. I derived so much satisfaction over this little task that it seems to me that collectors would like to hear about it, so I have included Dr. Milner's letter, and the photograph he sent me, in the colour section.

There was another special which particularly interested me. I was approached by D.C. Thomson & Co., Limited, the publishers, who asked if we would participate in a series of articles they were producing in their weekly publication of *Twinkle* - a picture paper specially for little girls.

The feature was to be called "Dainty Dollies - Costume Dolls to Cut Out and Keep." The first we made for them was a Swiss doll, which they called *Heidi*. A copy of the actual publication is included in the colour section.

Finally, there was a request from one of a large group of

Special Limited Editions.

Customer Exclusive Models.

Lady Mayoress presenting Claire Bloom with a Peggy Nisbet doll dressed as Juliet. Weston-super-Mare. 1960s.

companies - I think it was the Lever group at that time, to supply dolls for a self-liquidating promotion in connection with Izal toilet paper. My first reaction was one of horror. Our hand-made collectors' costume dolls to be used to advertise toilet paper! Perish the thought.

Then there were second thoughts. After all, I was running a business. A large company had come to us because we could supply them with a good reliable article. It would mean a very satisfactory amount of extra work which could easily be fitted into our production programme, and in the end it would be doll collectors who would apply for the dolls. So I accepted. The dolls were designed exclusively for Izal, so that they did

112

not interfere with our normal range for retail outlets, and we had an agreement whereby the name Peggy Nisbet was not associated with the promotion. There was a battle to obtain this concession because our name would have been of value to the Izal promotion, but finally they agreed to my terms.

There was a television commercial, the production of which I attended, but in which neither I nor the name of Nisbet participated. It took one whole day in the studio to shoot, but ended up as a two minute episode. Nowadays one would be pleased to have one's name associated with a television commercial. Famous designers and personalities are delighted to participate in this type of advertising, but this was about 15 to 20 years ago, when publicity of this kind was looked at askance. I have managed to find an old Izal toilet roll wrapper, which has been photographed and included in the colour section. It is the most amusing of our specials.

The exclusive Beatrix Potter soft toy range, which was my pride and joy, is described in Chapter XVI.

The famous actress Claire Bloom came to Weston to open our new swimming pool so we made a model of her dressed as Juliet, which was presented to her by the Lady Mayoress. Claire Bloom was that year appearing as Juliet in the Stratford-upon-Avon production of "Romeo and Juliet."

One of the most interesting models I have ever made should be included in this chapter. It is *The Yeoman Warder (Beefeater)* which was designed with the help and guidance of Sir Thomas Butler, the then Governor of The Tower of London, who checked and approved the prototype at every stage of development. Our first meeting was at the Governor's residence at The Tower of London in February 1969 when he paraded a Beefeater before us to show details of his uniform after which we returned to London for a meeting with Officers of the Commercial Experimental and Purchasing Department at the offices of the Ministry of Works. The display box itself was designed by The Ministry of Works and the model is made exclusively for The Tower of London under a contract which is renewed annually. The doll is not allowed to be sold in any shops or stores in Great Britain. However, permission has been granted for it to be exported throughout the remainder of the world, so is available for any stockists of Peggy Nisbet dolls overseas.

Every model sent to The Tower of London undergoes further stringent checks before being passed for sale, both at our factory and at The Tower of London itself, where a Yeoman Warder sits in his little hut examining every doll received from us, which he checks before passing it on to their souvenir shop.

It must have taken two years to get the model into production. For several months Alison and I paid numerous visits to the offices of The Ministry of Works to negotiate the contract. Once that was settled we had many more visits to The Tower of London. We examined again a set of clothes as worn by the Yeoman Warder, one of whom also acted as a model, and turned around whilst we took photographs, notes and sketches. Alison, Mabel Perry, Jean Hancock and I all went to The Tower on many occasions until finally permission was given for us to go into production.

At a later date the manufacturers of Beefeater Gin approached us and asked if we could supply them with a quantity of our "Ministry Beefeaters" as we call them, for a special project. They wanted a number of dolls to give to guests at an International Conference. Under our contract with the Ministry of Works we were not, of course, allowed to supply them but we asked if an exception could be made on this occasion. The Ministry agreed.

Original Nisbet Childhood Classics
models: Teddy Bear group.

Beatrix Potter group: Mrs. Tiggywinkle; Tom Kitten; Jemima Puddleduck: Peter Rabbit; Lady Mouse; Foxy Gentleman.

University of Bristol, Department of Psychology.

Telephone Bristol 24161

UNIVERSITY OF BRISTOL

DEPARTMENT OF PSYCHOLOGY
8-10 BERKELEY SQUARE
BRISTOL
BS8 1HH

Mrs. P.Nisbet,

Peggy Nisbet, Ltd.

27 ix 1971

Dear Mrs.Nisbet,

You may remember that three years ago you were kind enough to
supply me with some of your dolls, specially dressed to order by Mrs.Perry,
to help with some research that I was undertaking with coloured immigrant
children. The research is now completed and I have written about it in an
article published in last week's New Society. I am sending you a copy as I
thought you might be interested to read it. The research was extremely
successful and is to be the subject of a book I am writing for Penguin Books
in the near future. The dolls were a very important feature of the research
and contributed greatly to its success; I might add that they have been
universally admired by everyone who has seen them, not least the children
in the project. I am writing to let you know how significantly your efforts
contributed to the research, and how grateful I am for your kindness.

I have one further favour to ask, a rather less demanding one this time. I
have just been contacted by a colleague in Africa who hopes to do some similar
research to mine, on a rather simpler scale. Needless to say there is something
of a shortage of life-like dolls in Uganda, and it occurred to me that you might
be able to help. He simply wants 4 figures, 2 boys and 2girls like the ones I
had (see enclosed photos) and his wife will undertake to colour and dress them.
Would you be prepared to supply these? I would pay for them directly and he
could re-imburse me in due course. If, in addition, you could provide two 'blonde'
and two black female wigs, it would help them enormously in improvising life-like
hair styles. I really would be most grateful if you could help once again in
this way; perhaps you could let me know whether you could manage this.

Meanwhile, my very best wishes to yourself and Mrs.Perry,

Yours sincerely,

David Milner (Dr.)

114

Rag dolls - silk screen printed: B.B.C. "Watch with Mother" programmes "The Herbs" and "Pogles Wood." Dick Bruna characters.

Silk screen printed soft toys, circa 1970.

Healacraft bisque china dolls: V/850 *Monday's Girl* and
V/859 *Friday's Boy*.

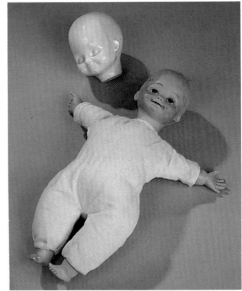

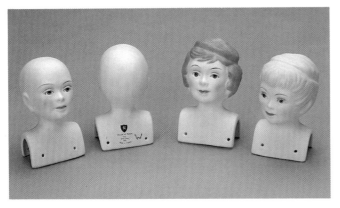

Healacraft bisque china heads.

RIGHT: Prototype of Peggy Nisbet's granddaughter, Felicity
(never in production). China bisque, 16in (41cm). Made as
"one or" by Bill and Martha Martin of Langley, Washington,
U.S.A.

Walt Disney characters:
Christopher Robin and
Pooh, Piglet, Kanga, Roo
and Eyeore.

Walt Disney. *Mary Poppins* - Topsy-turvey.

Walt Disney. *Mary Poppins* in Nanny's outdoor dress. *Mary Poppins* in white summer outfit.

Wooden Peg Tops and other dolls made from local beech.

Group of 6in (15cm) *Happy Dolls*.

1in (3cm) scale miniatures, fully-articulated.

EVERY THURSDAY   Price 7d.

No. 4 Feb. 17th, 1968

Twinkle

The NEW picture paper specially for little girls

FREE INSIDE

More pretty clothes
for your stand-up figure
of Twinkle.

"Twinkle" (Girls' picture paper) 1968, front cover. Reproduced by kind permission of D.C. Thomson & Co. Ltd.

Dainty Dollies
77

Costume dolls to
cut out and keep.

This lovely dolly is called Heidi. She comes from Switzerland, a country of high mountains and green valleys.

In many parts of Switzerland, jewellery and lace are made. Heidi's costume is trimmed with this lace, and her hair is held in place with silver pins.

Doesn't she look smart in her hat of plaited straw!

More lovely costume dolls in weeks to come.

This doll by Peggy Nisbet Ltd.

"Twinkle" (Girls' picture paper), page 6. Reproduced by kind permission of D.C. Thomson & Co. Ltd.

Izal promotion.

119

Sitting room, The Tower, Weston-super-Mare.

Peggy Nisbet and family, New Year's Day, 1986 at The Tower, Weston-super-Mare. Left to Right: Standing - Angus Nisbet (grandson); Jack Wilson (son-in-law); Peter Nisbet (son); Alison Wilson (daughter); James Fox (grandson); Felicity Wilson (granddaughter); Charlotte Fox (granddaughter); Andrew Nisbet (grandson); Anne Nisbet (Andrew's wife). Front Row: Alice Nisbet (granddaughter); Clementine Wilson (granddaughter); Peggy Nisbet; Mary Nisbet (daughter-in-law); William Nisbet Wilson (grandson).

Museums, Doll Collectors and Visits to the Tower

It would be interesting to write about the many Peggy Nisbet doll collections in Britain and the U.S.A. but there is only sufficient space for me to describe a few.

The first to be mentioned is our own Woodspring Museum, situated in Weston-super-Mare to whom, at their request, I have loaned my personal collection. It is a small museum which was only opened in 1975, but it attracts people from all over the country, and draws a large number of visitors throughout the year.

The wood block floor of the main courtyard belongs to the era when horses were stabled there. Later, in 1912, the Gaslight Company built its workshops around the old mews and remained in occupation until 1970, after which the building was converted into the existing museum.

The displays include an old chemist shop, a dentist's surgery, circa 1900, a dairy, jewellery and domestic items. The Victorians came to Weston-super-Mare, then a small village, for their seaside holidays, reaching a peak in the 1880s and 1890s. The town contains some excellent Victorian architecture of which my own home dating from the 1860s is an example.

There is a much older settlement called Worlebury on the hill overlooking Weston-super-Mare, where an Iron Age hill fort with solid drystone walls was built over 2000 years ago.

The transformation of the old gasworks into one of the most interesting little museums in the country was brought about almost entirely by the energy and creative ability of the Curator, Jane Evans, who has two equally energetic and creative assistants, Alec Coles and Sharon Poole. Between them they devise one superb exhibition after another throughout the year.

Recently I asked Jane to write me some notes about herself and her work, which appear below. From these you will see what a versatile curator we have here.

"I have worked in Museums for many years now, entering the profession as a trainee at Birmingham City Museum after graduating in Geography at Leicester University.

"My special interest has always been archaeology and after Birmingham I spent nine months working in Crete on Minoan pottery. Then I moved to Worthing Museum where my eyes were first opened to an interest in historic dolls and toys as a Museum subject. Mary Hillier discovered the collection in store there and many are featured in her book *Dolls and Dollmakers*. As a result of her guidance I wrote a catalogue of the Worthing Museum doll collection. Whilst there we staged a highly successful teddy bears' picnic, probably the first of those that were to follow.

"I then moved to Wales as Development Officer for the Council of Museums in Wales, travelling the country and offering advice to the small Museums. This was followed by a spell of six months in Australia where some weeks were spent working on a huge sheep station as a jilleroo. On my return I started work at Weston-super-Mare as Curator in July 1974. Here I am responsible for a local Museum serving a district with a population of 160,000, and an increased summer population of tourists. The displays are aimed to entertain as well as educate and reflect the history and activities of the area. Alec Coles the assistant curator is responsible for the natural history collections and Sharon Poole, museum assistant, for the costume and local history collections.

"Since re-establishing the Museum in the old converted Gaslight Company workshops in 1975, new galleries have been regularly opened. In 1982 it seemed a great idea to invite Peggy Nisbet to place her personal collection of Peggy Nisbet dolls and the Carlberg legacy on display in a special room in the Museum.

"Perhaps it will be no surprise to learn that a recent visitors' questionnaire revealed the Peggy Nisbet doll collection was the most popular gallery in the whole Museum."

Jane, Alec and Sharon were of invaluable assistance in mounting my own display in the museum, and it is due to them, and not to me, that such a good display has been built in a comparatively small space.

My exhibition held in association with the Woodspring District Council was launched at a Private View on Wednesday, 18th August 1983. A photograph taken at the reception shows the existing Mayor, Dun Brewer and wife, with the ex-mayor Jim Dickson who had been most helpful previously after our old factory had been burned to the ground, and I applied to the council to buy some land on the new Oldmixon Trading Estate upon which to build our new factory.

Among the many photographs taken in the museum is one showing Dennis Thatcher accepting a doll of his wife, Prime Minister Margaret Thatcher, which I was asked to present to him on the occasion of a visit he paid to Weston-super-Mare in aid of the disabled. I was most impressed because he wrote a letter of thanks in his own handwriting instead of a typewritten acknowledgment. A very courteous gesture. He told me his wife was better looking than our model of her!

The collage which I have hung in the museum and of which a photograph appears in this book, will be interesting to collectors, showing as it does every process of dressing a doll from start to finish (Chapter XVIII). The three strips at the bottom of the collage are three short lengths of mohair (auburn, dark brown and white) with which, when opened out, we make our hair styles, arranging and glueing them straight onto the doll's head.

Doll firm works on after £50,000 blaze

Left: The pall of smoke which hung over the burning workshops. Above: A fireman hosing the roof of the building from the top of the turntable ladder.

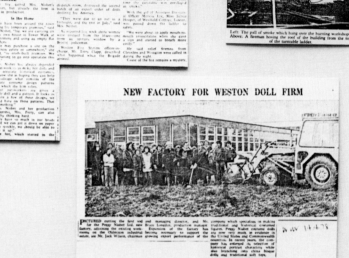

NEW FACTORY FOR WESTON DOLL FIRM

Woodspring Museum: Press cuttings.

THE STORY OF THE COMPANY

Woodspring Museum: Collage showing Peggy Nisbet presenting Margaret Thatcher doll to her husband, Dennis Thatcher, on visit to Weston in connection with the disabled, together with his letter of thanks. 1983.

View of exterior Woodspring Museum, Weston-super-Mare.

Woodspring Museum: Interior. Sharon Poole, Jane Evans (Curator) and Alec Coles.

Mildred Carlberg.

This case contains part of the Collection of over
300 dolls bequeathed to Peggy Nisbet by

Mildred E. Carlberg

of

Los Angeles, U.S.A.

who died in August 1980.

Mildred Carlberg was a very early collector of
Nisbet dolls and expressed the wish that as many
collectors as possible should have the pleasure
of seeing and enjoying her collection.

THE LEGACY

Woodspring Museum: Millie Carlberg's collection bequeathed to Peggy Nisbet. 1980.

Woodspring Museum: Opening of Exhibition 18 August 1983. Mayor of Weston, Dan Brewer and wife; Peggy Nisbet, Ex-Mayor of Weston, Jim Dickson and wife.

Woodspring Museum: Peggy Nisbet with some of her private collection of ethnic dolls, 1983.

Finally, one of the most interesting corners of the room contains a cabinet in which I have put much of the collection of Millie Carlberg.

There is a sad story attached to this. For some years I received numbers of letters from a William Carlberg of Los Angeles. He wrote enquiring about different dolls, which new ones were going to be produced, where he could buy models he was unable to obtain, and a variety of requests for information. I was always intrigued by his keen interest in our dolls, and always assumed he was himself a collector.

One day I received a telephone call from Los Angeles. It was Bill Carlberg himself. He told me that his wife, Mildred, had died from cancer the previous day and her dying wish was that her collection of 300 Peggy Nisbet dolls should be shipped to me, if possible, for other collectors to see and admire them.

It appeared that week after week he had arranged for a doll to arrive by post to add to the collection which must have given her so much pleasure and comfort in her last illness.

I contacted my friends, Ken and Martha Kuehn, who live in Los Angeles, and they were kind enough to arrange for the packing and shipment of the dolls to England. They went to a great deal of trouble to do this, and I was so grateful to them. Ken Kuehn was the representative in Los Angeles for our Agents, Reeves International, Inc., of whom I have written in another chapter. A photograph of Ken and Martha appears in the book.

Tragically, a few months later I received another telephone call from Los Angeles. It was from Millie Carlberg's mother saying that Bill, too, had died of cancer.

What a sad story of such a loving couple.

The Bethnal Green Museum of Childhood in London, which is a branch of the Victoria and Albert Museum, is visited by most doll collectors who come to Great Britain.

The curator of dolls at the museum is Caroline Georgina Goodfellow, a Canadian who came to London for a year, found enough time to get involved with dolls and decided to stay. As curator of the Bethnal Green Museum, she is in charge of the largest collection of dolls and dolls' houses in England.

Her main duties centre on the permanent exhibition of some 1500 dolls which range in date from 1670 to the present day. She has written many articles on dolls as well as one major book.

Caroline's other duties range from lecturing to interested parties, meeting foreign visitors to the museum (many of whom come from the U.S.A.) and visiting other doll areas and countries on fact-finding and lecture tours. She regularly visits the United States.

The leaflet which Caroline sent me, from which she said I could quote, says:

"DOLLS — Archaeologists have dug up dolls from many ancient civilizations, but our collection begins with wooden dolls of early modern Europe, notably an English doll

125

(c.1680), finely clothed and with lace head-dress, that is said to have belonged to a follower of the Old Pretender."

I am honoured to have my china bisque model of Queen Victoria displayed in such august company.

There are collections of my dolls, some larger and some smaller, in many of the museums in Europe and America and there are literally hundreds of personal collections which I have seen and would love to mention. Space, alas, is my enemy. Bob and Jean Hill of New Jersey, whom I have mentioned before, have a large collection, as also has her friend, Mrs. Halberg, whose collection fills her house. Jacquie Watt also of New Jersey, Eileen Halpern of Cincinnati, Ohio, and many, many more whom I have met on my travels have Peggy Nisbet collections, some of them running into hundreds.

About 20 miles from Weston, in South Wales, Mavis Hunt has over 200 of our dolls, displayed in groups, and all of them displayed in one room. They fill her whole life. A snapshot which I took in her home, when she was wearing her traditional Welsh costume, is here reproduced.

Most of the groups of doll enthusiasts who have visited my home from the U.S.A. have collections of our dolls.

John Knox's house in The Royal Mile, Edinburgh, always has a large permanent exhibit.

Those of my collector friends whom I have not mentioned must forgive me for omitting their names.

Many hundreds of collectors have visited me at my home, after or before having had a tour of the factory. My home is an octagonal building, an old Water Tower, which I have converted for my own use.

Sometimes it is individuals who come, many from the U.S.A. who are on holiday in this country, whilst others come in groups or on organized coach trips.

One year in which we had a particularly large number of visitors was 1977. In April collectors came to see us with Catherine MacLaren, with whom I had discussed the project when I saw her in San Diego the previous year. In May we had another party of 20 collectors headed by Dorothy Coleman and her daughter, Ann. Thereafter we had a continuous stream of visitors. After touring the factory they all came to The Tower for a buffet lunch, when I always tried to include traditional British food. My visitors invariably appeared to like orange and other fruit squashers, which are different from American soft drinks. Other favourite food seemed to be cold veal and ham pie, sausage rolls and, as a last course, sherry trifle. We also made a trifle without sherry for those who did not like alcohol. Bill and Martha Martin brought over groups on two occasions as also did Jacquie Watt.

Thirty-four members of The Letitia Penn Doll Club came to tour the factory on 24th May — they had lunch with me afterwards and we had a most enjoyable day.

There are many, many others whom I cannot mention due to lack of space but I think of them often and hope that they will continue to visit me.

Included in this chapter is a photograph of my sitting room at The Tower, which many will remember as we all gathered here for our pre-luncheon aperitif.

Caroline Goodfellow and Peggy Nisbet.

Doll Collectors — Eleanor McBride, Antoinette Ollinger, Peggy Nisbet and Maxime Oliver, 1975.

Doll Collectors — Mr. & Mrs. Halberg and Peggy Nisbet, 1983.

Doll Collector — Mavis Hunt, 1986.

Doll Collector — Cindy DeMeane, mid 1970s.

PARADE OF HISTORY

—Cindy DeMeane of Transmission Design collects character dolls and says her hobby strengthens her knowledge of history. Here she shows her Elizabethean collection which includes Henry VIII and his six wives. This part of her 35-doll collection was acquired during historical tours of England.

Doll Collectors — Mary Rainford and Elizabeth Grove.

Eileen Halpern and Peggy Nisbet, 1982.

Mimi Halpern, 1982.

Visit of Edyth Casita to The Tower and factory, 1977. Entertained by Peggy Nisbet and Shrubbery Doll Club.

Visit of Dorothy Coleman's group to The Tower and factory, May 1977.

Visit of Dorothy Coleman's group to The Tower and factory, May 1977.

Bill and Martha Martin's group outside The Tower.

Bill and Martha Martin's group luncheon at The Tower.

Sitting room at The Tower.

U.F.D.C. and
N.A.M.E. Conventions

No-one who has not had the privilege of attending the annual conventions organized by the U.F.D.C. (United Federation of Doll Clubs, Inc.) and other conventions, can possibly imagine the magnitude of the undertaking, and the two or three years' work involved for the "host" club.

For everyone attending one of the conventions, it is an unforgettable experience. I have been privileged to attend many during the last decade, and each one was a memorable occasion.

One of the fascinating things about them is that although they all have the same overall objectives, every city hosting the event has a different theme and attitude, so there is constant variety. Above all, there is always the spirit, the friendliness, the exchange of ideas, the competitions, workshops, banquets. How the organisers cram it all into a few days, I shall never know.

It would be interesting to look up my diaries and write about each one, but alas my enemy, lack of space, rears up its head.

One which was not necessarily better than the others, is memorable from my point of view because I was able to attend both the U.F.D.C. and the N.A.M.E. (National Association of Miniature Enthusiasts). This was in 1981 in St. Louis when they ran concurrently in the same city.

Bob Marshall, to whom I have referred elsewhere, was there, and also his wife, Barbara, together with their attractive and competent daughter, Barbie-Jo. I shared a stand with them at the N.A.M.E. Convention in order to exhibit my miniatures.

My journey did not provide a good start. When I should have been helping to set up our stand, I was stranded at the Chicago airport, where I missed my connection to St. Louis. At midnight I was still there. My luggage was lost, elevators were not working, my purse was stolen, none of the airport staff knew what was happening and, to crown it all, when the plane for St. Louis finally arrived, there were no seats available, although my reservation had been booked through to its destination.

By this time I was almost in a state of collapse but a TWA official saw me sitting disconsolately and took pity on me. He found my luggage and wangled a first class seat from somewhere at economy class rate, into which I sank thankfully.

The two conventions more than made up for my frustrating journey. The Marshalls had set up the miniatures and I was able to get around and see some of the lovely exhibits. Some of them were exquisite: no words of mine can describe the intricacy and the beauty of the work.

U.F.D.C. Convention at Waldorf-Astoria Hotel, New York, Peggy Nisbet and Dee Rabey of Granite City, Illinois, 1979.

The evenings remain in my memory. After the salesrooms closed we met together. One night we had an enjoyable dinner party with Bob, Barbara and Barbie-Jo Marshall, when we were joined by Mary Beth and Beth Benore, the well-known mother and daughter team who run Hobby Center Toys whose main shop is in Toledo, Ohio. The next night we had cocktails in my room, then dinner with the Marshalls. This time we were joined by Mary Harris Francis. Barbara Marshall and Mary Harris Francis have spent the last decade in organising their Museum of Miniatures and Dolls' Houses in Kansas City which is now open to the public. The museum, the result of so many years of hard work by its two devoted creators, contains a fabulous collection including the many custom-made pieces of furniture commissioned from famous craftsmen by Barbara and her late husband, Bob.

The U.F.D.C. convention followed that of the N.A.M.E. and as I was due to give a lecture, I was on tenterhooks until my talk was over. Lectures as such, comprising a series of slides with commentaries, do not appeal to me. I prefer to talk away, without notes, just saying what comes into my head.

131

Jacqueline Watt.

U.F.D.C. Convention dinner, Washington, D.C., 1980.

My programme was entitled "English Dolls." This had been quite difficult to prepare because there are so few old English dolls, most of the well-known antique dolls being of French or German origin. However, with the help of some of our doll archivists and assistance from the Staffordshire Potteries, I managed to collect some interesting facts, in addition to which I had some new slides taken which were quite unusual. Other slides were loaned to me by Faith Eaton, Caroline Goodfellow (Curator of the Bethnal Green Museum), Marguerite Fawdry of Pollock's Toy Shop in London (who kindly arranged for a photographer to take some shots of old, previously unknown dolls on my behalf) and Mary Hillier, who is always so generous with her help and advice.

I had expected perhaps a few hundred people to attend but when I opened the door to go into the lecture hall, I nearly turned back and went away again. The hall was packed and I was told there were over 1000 in the audience. However, it all seemed to go off well and appeared to be successful.

After the convention ended, I stayed on for another 24 hours in St. Louis to see the sights and shops, buy some jazz records and call on an old friend, Glen Munson, the Toy Buyer of the Famous Barr store. It was his 24th wedding anniversary, so they asked me to their party which I enjoyed enormously. I also spent one evening taking a trip on the Huck Finn River Steamer, where there was dinner and Dixieland music.

Most of the conventions I attended on my own but Jack accompanied me to the one in Denver, whilst Alison came with me to Kansas City in 1982 and to San Diego in 1983.

At San Diego Jacqueline Watt and I had reserved a stand jointly. The hours were long and we were obliged to miss some of the events because of this, but it was very interesting. So many people visited the rooms and it was an ideal place in which to meet old friends. The weather was perfect and there was always time for a dip in the swimming pool. It was such a joy to have Alison as a companion. One of my legs, in which I had a thrombosis, was painful but she and Jacquie did all the hard work, so I was able to sit down for much of the time.

Jacquie and I first met in a lift in the Metropole Hotel, Brighton, while attending one of our few British Doll conventions named "Doll 77." It was here that Jacquie bought her first Peggy Nisbet doll, which was our bone china model of Queen Victoria. Her number was 451 of the Limited Edition of 500. The following week she came to lunch with me at The Tower, and I introduced her to Jack and Alison, who took her round the factory.

In 1980 Jacquie met me at the Philadelphia airport, and I stayed with her and her husband, Philip, at their home in Waretown, New Jersey, prior to my attendance at the Wannamaker Doll Show, where I was the guest of the store.

We met again in 1981 at the Second Doll Symposium at Meredith College in Raleigh, North Carolina, where I was the guest speaker. The same year we shared a booth in the sales room of the U.F.D.C. Convention in St. Louis.

Our most recent meeting was in March 1985 when Jacquie brought a tour group to England and I invited them to luncheon after which they visited the factory.

Jacquie and her husband, Phil, have entertained me at their home on several occasions, and made me very welcome. They have driven me around the countryside and given me a wonderful time at their waterside home in New Jersey. They have become good friends.

The 1980 convention in Washington, D.C., was beautifully presented and was one of the most interesting and

Peggy Nisbet and Edna Hunze at U.F.D.C. Convention, Denver, 1978.

successful I have attended despite the fact that the organisers had to cope with enormous problems. Major alterations were taking place in the hotel in which it was held, and there were workmen everywhere. One had to step over cables, avoid such hazards as cement mixers and huge equipment, whilst all the time one could hear hammering and explosive noises of all kinds.

Bettyanne Twigg and her team did a superb job, backed up as usual by Dorothy Coleman with her daughters, Ann and Jane, together with members of the Dollology Club of Washington of which I am a member.

At the Denver convention in 1978 I was accompanied by Jack Wilson. We had an exhausting journey, travelling to Denver from London, via Seattle, but as usual enjoyed meeting all our friends.

So many U.F.D.C. officials have made us welcome, Candace Doelman, Beryl Knoblauch, Shirley Buchholz and Ralph Griffith to name but a few. Patty Marchal entertained us at early morning breakfasts, whilst Dorothy Coleman was always there to give us a helping hand and advice.

In writing this chapter I have re-lived the many U.F.D.C. functions, and the squeals of excitement as the lucky prize-winners at each table received their awards will always remain in my memory.

How fortunate are those of us who have had the privilege of attending these gatherings.

Peggy Nisbet and Jack Wilson at
U.F.D.C. Convention, Denver, 1978.

Peggy Nisbet, Barbara Marshall and
Alison Wilson at the Miniature
Museum, Kansas City, 1982.

Doll Collecting In Great Britain

Doll collecting in the United Kingdom is still in its infancy compared with the serious collecting which has been done in the U.S.A. over the last few decades. Thirty years ago anyone collecting antique dolls was laughed at and regarded as somewhat of a freak: quite definitely an eccentric.

Mrs. Nerea de Clifford had been a doll lover since her childhood and when she was an adult, she continued to collect dolls, had the courage of her convictions, and decided to form a doll club with some of her friends. Thus The Doll Club of Great Britain was born.

Two or three years ago Moira Garland wrote about the formation and growth of the club, and she has given me permission to re-print her article.

Irene Blair Hickman was an early member and Gwen White, who wrote so knowledgeably about dolls, was the archivist. Vivien Graham Greene was the President. Faith Eaton attended the very first meeting, and is still actively involved to-day.

Another doll enthusiast was Kay Desmond whose shop in Kensington has been visited by so many. Her magnificent collection has been seen by thousands at Sudeley Castle, Gloucestershire. Mary Hillier is an enthusiastic collector and a famous author.

They are all world-famous authorities on doll collecting, although their numbers are few.

As well as collecting dolls, many of the members have dolls' house collections, one of the most famous being Faith Eaton's, which is housed in her lovely old Victorian home in London. Gillian Kernon, the club's Honorary Secretary, has an interesting collection of dolls' houses in Clevedon, which is only a few miles away from my own home.

Vivien Graham Greene has a collection of 100 pre-1890 dolls. She also has a collection of about 50 antique dolls' houses. She keeps the latter in The Rotunda, which she had built in her garden and to which she invites visitors during the summer months. The houses have genuine antique furniture, china, silver, and so forth of the period.

It is a matter of great regret to me that I have been so little involved in The Doll Club of Great Britain. For so many years I have attended U.F.D.C. Conventions in the U.S.A., and yet rarely do I participate in our own meetings and functions, but business has taken me so often to the States and all my time in this country was devoted to the running of the business. I hope that now I am no longer so involved in the factory, I may be able to get to the London meetings. I am looking forward to doing this.

Five years ago I formed our own small Shrubbery Doll Club in Weston-super-Mare. We were proud to be the first British Member of The United Federation of Doll Clubs, Inc., of the U.S.A. We meet monthly at each other's houses, and raise funds which we use to buy mohair jointed Teddy Bears. These are distributed to terminally ill children or children in unhappy circumstances who have been suggested to us by hospitals, nurses and those caring for them.

Amongst other doll clubs are The Heart of England, Lakeland Plangon Club (founder, Mary Doughty), Worcester Doll Club and Sussex Doll Club.

Doll collecting in the United Kingdom is growing rapidly, and collectors come from all over the world to attend the London auctions at Sothebys, Christies and other sale rooms, so maybe one day we shall have conventions and other doll functions on a larger scale, but it is not the nature of the British people generally to take their hobbies too seriously, and I suspect we shall go on in our own leisurely way just enjoying our collections without the commercialism and competitiveness which can sometimes detract from this rewarding and friendly hobby.

THIRTY ENTHUSIASTIC YEARS . . .

Moira Garland recalls 30 years of commitment by a dedicated few that has developed into a countrywide organisation with 300 members.

Above: Mrs. Gillian Kernon, the club's honorary secretary, pictured at the 30th Anniversary party and exhibition held in June this year. Left: Flashback to 1978 - club founder member Mrs. Nerea de Clifford cuts the 25th Anniversary cake at St. Mary Abbott's Hall, Kensington.

Forty years ago doll collecting in England was in its infancy. Little interest was shown in antique dolls and the prices were correspondingly low, early wax dolls in their original clothes could be bought for about £5 and a Dream Baby was valued at around £2 to £3. Very little was written about the subject and one of the first books, which came from the States where the hobby was a great deal more popular, was Dolls of Yesterday written by Eleanor St. George, published in 1946.

In July 1953 a small band of enthusiasts gathered together in a house in Holland Park, London at the invitation of Mrs. Nerea de Clifford to consider the formation of a new club. Mrs. de Clifford had been an avid doll collector since her youth. Her interest started, as it does in so many cases, with a gift of dolls which had belonged in her childhood to an old family friend. So far as was known the new club was to be the first of its kind in the world, and so the Doll Club of Great Britain was launched.

Originally there were eight committee members, Mrs. Graham Green was President and Mrs. de Clifford was Hon. Sec. and Treasurer. The annual subscription was 5/- (25p) for a full member and 2/6d (12½p) for an Associate. The aims of the Club were, and still are, to ensure the preservation of old and interesting dolls, dolls' houses and accessories, to encourage the production of good modern dolls and to subscribe to recognised charities. Several names were suggested as a collective term for doll collectors and after some discussion Plangonologist was decided upon. Someone discovered the Greek word "Plangon" meaning "a wax model of the human figure made for the amusement of children", and this was the name given to the Club's quarterly news-letter. I have yet to hear anyone refer to themselves as a Plangonologist, but it may come and certainly one member called their new house Plangon Villa!

When the club started, the newsletter was just one sheet, but this has now grown to a small magazine of about 20 pages, as yet unillustrated, and is available only to members. Originally there were two types of members, Full and Associate, with Full members paying a slightly higher subscription. The latter was intended for people who lived outside London and were unable to attend many meetings. This was changed in 1981 to only one type of membership and a yearly subscription of £4 for all members was introduced with an entrance fee of 50p for each meeting. For many years the mainstay

of the Club was Mrs. Vivien Greene, so well-known for her wonderful collection of dolls' houses, who acted as President, Hon. Secretary and Editor of Plangon, but in December 1974 she retired. As it was decided that no one could adequately replace her a new format for the Committee was decided upon, consisting of an Hon. Secretary, Hon. Treasurer, Membership Secretary and several committee members, any of whom could conduct the meetings and edit Plangon. From this will be seen the magnitude of the task which Mrs. Greene tackled virtually single-handed, and fortunately for us all she agreed to become the Patron.

In September 1974 the first Doll Club Convention ever organised in Great Britain or Europe was held at Portmeirion in North Wales. Many visitors from the States and Europe attended and it was voted a great success. Compared to the huge Conventions in the States it was a relatively small affair, but most people seemed to think that this was an advantage and created a very friendly atmosphere. This is to date the major event run by the Club but there are many others.

In 1978 the Doll Club of Great Britain celebrated its 25th Anniversary with a whole week of events, starting with a birthday celebration at St. Mary Abbott's Hall in Kensington. Mrs. de Clifford was there and cut a special

birthday cake, and Mrs. Greene as Patron spoke of the 25 years of the Doll Club and its aims and ambitions for the future. Then followed a whole week of enjoyment with such events as a Jubilee luncheon at a London Hotel; an evening reception at Christie's where one was able to view the dolls and toys which were coming up for sale the following day, whilst sampling delicious food and drink; a visit to the Bethnal Green Museum and several visits to private collections. The Club usually has a meeting of some kind every month. Mostly the meetings are London orientated but very many other activities take place further afield, such as visits to private collections, museums etc. and members often offer hospitality to view their own collections. The notice is inserted in Plangon and those who wish to attend write for an invitation. The number of guests is usually limited depending on the size of the accommodation available.

To mark the Club's 30th Anniversary in June this year there was a whole day devoted to demonstrations and lectures; the usual Christmas party will be held in December, and once, if not twice a year there is a Fair or Flea Market with stalls manned by members and this is one event to which the public is admitted. It is from the proceeds of these Fairs that a donation is given to a chosen charity.

The Club now has some 300 members and by organising exhibitions and displays of dolls, with lectures, expeditions, competitions and discussion groups it enables its members to share and increase their knowledge.

Information can be obtained from the Hon. Secretary, Mrs. Gillian Kernon, 5 The Avenue, Clevedon, Avon. BS21 7EB on receipt of a s.a.e. The yearly subscription, which includes Plangon, is £4 for all members in the U.K. Outside the U.K. the subscription is $10.

B.T.M.A. Dinner, 1959. Mary, Peter, Peggy & Alison Nisbet.

B.T.M.A. Dinner, 1976. Jack & Alison Wilson, Mary and Peter Nisbet, Jean & Roger Swinburne-Johnson, Peggy Nisbet, Bill and Thören Fieldhouse.

The Silver Jubilee Of Queen Elizabeth II

—————————1977—————————

Silver Jubilee year provided an occasion for great celebration and pageantry: for three years I had been engaged on the designs of models to commemorate the occasion, and it is impossible to describe in detail the vast amount of research required.

My first china bisque doll, made in 1952 to commemorate The Coronation in 1953 had been a model of H.M. Queen Elizabeth II. On that occasion I had been obliged to make an inspired guess as to the design of the Coronation dress and robes. Here 25 years later, when celebrating The Queen's Silver Jubilee and my own Silver Jubilee as a doll maker, an opportunity presented itself to design a coronation model with accurate reproductions of the dress, robes and vestments worn at the ceremony. It was the most exciting and enjoyable of all my projects.

The doll itself was no great problem. Ron Cameron did the modelling and Roger Turrell, who was by this time engaged in moulding Peggy Nisbet bone china bisque models for us, using our own formula, started work on the moulds and casting. The formula and processes of making our bisque dolls are described in another chapter.

The problems were to obtain details of the coronation dress, the vestments used in the coronation ceremony, and the Royal Arms. The most difficult was inevitably going to be producing the latter in miniature, particularly in the reproduction of true heraldic colours.

The Lord Chamberlain announced that the Queen had been pleased to approve of the rules governing the use of The Royal Arms being temporarily relaxed to allow their use on approved souvenirs of her Majesty's Silver Jubilee.

My first job, then, was to obtain the approval of The Lord Chamberlain to my proposed model. This meant a visit to St. James's Palace, London, as had been the case 25 years earlier, when I made my first doll.

Having obtained the necessary permission, the next step was to obtain details of The Royal Arms and the coronation dress, and to decide how to reproduce them.

The necessary information regarding The Royal Arms was obtained, but now began the task of reproducing them accurately and in miniature.

Sue Worth was given drawings and coloured illustrations of The Royal Arms. She scaled these down and painted the design on paper. We sought and obtained the necessary go-ahead: then we had to decide upon the method of reproduction. Jack Wilson approached his old company, Letraset, who made several trials to print the design onto the appropriate cloth. First tests were not at all good. As I had anticipated, it was difficult to obtain the clear heraldic colours required. Finally, however, Jack's perseverance was crowned with success and a superlatively good reproduction was obtained.

The final problem was the coronation dress and vestments. I cannot print a copy of Her Majesty wearing the coronation dress in this book because of copyright. I have, however, had a photograph taken of our material. It shows the detail very well, and if readers are interested, they should compare it with postcards or photographs of The Queen in her coronation dress.

The cloth for the dress and the vestments was woven by Mr. Ungar who is one of the most talented designers and producers of brocade in the country.

Both Mr. Ungar and I together, and separately, visited The Tower of London where the robes were on display. Government and Tower of London officials gave us every possible assistance, even opening up the cases to enable us to walk round the exhibits. Mr. Ungar went to Switzerland to get the Jacquards made which were required to weave the brocades, and the result was superb.

The Nisbet bone china bisque and leather 8in (20cm) models were sold direct to collectors by Tower Treasures Ltd. and in addition to the coronation model consisted of:

1) *H.M. Queen Elizabeth II* in formal Jubilee gown sitting in accurate replica of gilt upholstered period chair
2) *H.R.H. Prince Philip*
3) *The King of Arms*

For many years Mr. Ungar designed for me, in miniature, brocades inspired by Elizabethan or Medieval fabrics, reproducing the colours of the period as far as he was able with to-day's dyes and cloths. We met regularly, usually in London, where we would sit in the lounge of The English Speaking Union, of which I am a member, or in a London hotel, where we were somewhat of a curiosity as swatch after swatch of trials were brought out and discussed and spread out on the coffee table in front of us.

The creation of the coronation dress fabric is worthy of mention, and a close-up photograph of a section of the cloth appears in the coronation colour page. It is a unique brocade and must be the only authentic and totally accurate miniature reproduction in the world.

In addition to a coronation dressed doll, I wanted to reproduce the vestments used during the coronation ceremony. These consisted of the white Colobium Sindeonis, which is a sleeveless garment, not unlike a bishop's rochet; a

Queen Elizabeth II. Coronation dress. Designed for 1977 Silver Jubilee.

Queen Elizabeth II. Doll to commemorate Silver Jubilee 1977. Designed from official photograph.

Supertunica, or Close Pall, which is a robe of cloth of gold lined with crimson silk, together with a sword belt, which is also known as the girdle. John Lewin, whose work is already described in the book, modelled the coronation chair, which is sometimes called King Edward's Chair. King Edward I ordered it to be made to contain the Stone of Scone, which he captured from the Scots in 1296. This chair has been used in every coronation since that of Edward II in 1308.

The model I designed depicts Her Majesty arriving at Westminster Abbey wearing the coronation dress and the crimson velvet robes of a Peer of Parliament.

The full coronation ceremony is too long to describe in this book, but there are many publications which give a detailed story of the history and pageantry of the occasion, and for those interested in the subject they provide fascinating reading. I will merely give a short description.

Very briefly, the ceremony consists of the sovereign arriving at Westminster Abbey wearing the State crimson robe, after which he or she is presented to the people gathered in the Abbey, amongst whom are the royal family and Peers and Peeresses of the Realm, in full ceremonial dress. The sovereign is then acclaimed by the congregation, and this is followed by the administration of the Oath in which the sovereign swears to govern according to the laws, customs and religion of the country.

The sovereign sits on the Chair of State and the service of Holy Communion begins. Then the soverign moves to the coronation chair (King Edward's Chair). Holy oil is poured into the annointing spoon and the Archbishop touches the sovereign with it on the hands, breast and head. The annointing gives the sovereign claim to the royal title, and the ceremony continues with the investment with the royal robes as described above.

Coronation chair made by John Lewin.

Queen Elizabeth II and *Prince Philip*. Silver Jubilee models, 1977.

The Royal Herald, Jubilee model, 1977.

After receiving all the royal vestments and ornaments, there comes the supreme moment when the Archbishop of Canterbury places St. Edward's Crown on the sovereign's head. As he is doing this the people cry "God Save the King (or Queen)." The Princes, Princesses, Peers and Peeresses and the Kings of Arms put on their coronets and the trumpets are sounded.

After prayers the enthronement takes place. The sovereign goes to the raised throne, which faces the altar, and is "lifted up" into it by the Archbishop, Bishops and Peers and enthroned.

After the benediction the sovereign, still wearing St.

Edward's Crown descends from the throne. St. Edward's crown is very heavy and weighs about five pounds, so it is replaced by the lighter and better known Imperial State Crown.

The Sovereign then leaves the Abbey. St. Edward's Crown is not used again until the next coronation.

The doll was modelled by Ronald Cameron, whose work has already been described in an earlier chapter.

In the standard Peggy Nisbet styrene range we made a special Jubilee set of *Queen Elizabeth II* in an orchid pink gown and "diamond" tiara standing beside *Prince Philip* in his naval uniform and a *Royal Herald* in a specially designed box.

Rabbit, *Jubilee Lion, Jubilee Bear,* 1977.

Details of the Queen's dress were taken from the official Jubilee photograph.

The most interesting models in the Jubilee range were the perfect replicas of *The King of Arms* and the *Royal Herald* wearing Court Dress over which is worn the traditional tabard bearing The Royal Arms. They are unique models.

Officers-of-Arms, under the generic name of Heralds, have formed part of the establishment of the sovereign from very early times. Our models were produced with the assistance and co-operation of The College of Heralds.

Other Jubilee models in the standard range were *The Queen's Page* who carried the train of her robe, *The Mistress of the Robes*, a title usually bestowed upon a Duchess, and the *Earl Marshall*, hereditary Marshall of England, responsible for all large ceremonies, the most important of which is the Coronation.

It took over three years to research and produce the Silver Jubilee models, but it was an absorbing task.

The Silver Jubilee range was announced in our Newsletter No. 3 dated 3rd December 1976, and was produced in 1977.

There is frequently confusion over the date of The Queen's Silver Jubilee. Her Majesty ascended the throne upon the death of her father in 1952, but her coronation took place in 1953. Our models were designed and produced in 1977; they were to commemorate the official Silver Jubilee year of 1977.

As my own Silver Jubilee as a doll maker fell the same year, it was decided to celebrate it by holding a reception at The English Speaking Union in Mayfair, London, in November 1977 to which we invited old friends, buyers, suppliers and colleagues.

It was a happy and, for me, a very nostalgic occasion.

The large beautifully proportioned reception room with its old panelling and Adam fireplace was a perfect setting for the event. We had a buffet lunch with wines and light

Jubilee Bear, 1977.

refreshments, and around the walls were mounted displays of all the dolls in our current range, the pièce de résistance being the 1978 Jubilee range which was being shown for the first time.

For the occasion a wine coloured silk gown with a full length matching velvet cloak and small wisp of a hat with soft osprey feathers was designed and made for me by Cordell, the London couturier. The ensemble was subsequently reproduced in miniature on a doll modelled by Ron Cameron. I have been told that it is the first time that a doll maker has made a doll of herself. I do not know if this is true, but if so, I am not surprised because it is acutely embarrassing to display and sell such an item. I could never bring myself to encourage anyone to buy the model, although it became immensely popular as a unique collectors' item because of the occasion for which it was made. As Robert Burns says:

O Wad some Pow'r the giftie gie us
To see oursels as others see us

Well, the doll of myself gave me this power, and I must say that I was somewhat disconcerted at my witchlike face. Moreoever, it was very difficult to dress because the full size velvet cloak had several yards of rich velvet lined with silk, and it was impossible to gather so much material into the shoulder of a 7in (18cm) model and this prevented the classic line being shown to advantage.

Graham Wiltshire took some excellent photographs of the groups of dolls on display together with shots of some of our guests; many of these are reproduced in this book.

One of our oldest customers will be well-known to many collectors who read this book and we were delighted to see him at our Silver Jubilee Reception.

Basil George lives in Jersey in a house with a long terraced garden sloping down to a beautiful bay. The view from his windows is magnificent.

Basil sold our dolls in his delightful toy and gift shop situated in the centre of St. Helier. In the early sixties he was looking around for something to do, and came across a toy shop for sale - so he took it. He had a loyal staff who became totally involved in the merchandise, and kept attractive window displays of dolls which were a great attraction for visitors to the island.

Long before he bought the shop he had seen and admired Peggy Nisbet dolls as being authentic miniature reproductions of historical characters and costumes: for Basil is interested in the theatre, music and the arts, as well as being a sports enthusiast. He was impressed with the workmanship and decided to visit the B.T.M.A. International Toy Fair which, in the sixties, was held in Brighton. It was here that we first met. He has been a good customer and friend ever since and comes to visit us regularly.

Whilst his staff looked after the shop Basil became involved in supplying the needs of doll collectors all over the world and personally wrote to them in reply to their orders and letters. He started this mail order business by accident. A New Zealand girl working as a hotel receptionist in Jersey bought one of *Henry VIII's wives* to send home and Basil offered to pack and post it. He then produced a price list and spent £5 on an advertisement in a New Zealand magazine which produced several customers. He then extended his activities by advertising in **Doll Reader**®, which resulted in many new customers in the U.S.A.

Silver Jubilee Reception, November 1977. Miss Locke (Hamleys' doll buyer), Brian Griffin (Hamleys' Managing Director), Jack Wilson (House of Nisbet, Chairman and Managing Director).

Silver Jubilee Reception, November 1977. Stan Murphy (owner of Stanleys Gift Shop, Castle Hill, Windsor, one of the earliest stockists of Peggy Nisbet dolls), Peggy Nisbet.

Silver Jubilee Reception, November 1977. Peggy Nisbet and Cyril Stephens, Managing Director of Frederick Warne & Co., Ltd., publishers and licence holders of Beatrix Potter books.

Recently the lease of the shop expired. Basil decided not to re-open it in new premises but he continues to supply his mail order collectors from his home, as he enjoys continuing his correspondence with them.

Apart from the dolls, he is now very much occupied with raising funds to run the local hospice which provides specialised nursing care and accommodation for the terminally ill, usually cancer patients, allowing them to spend their remaining days in peace and comfort near their families. The picture shows him, right, receiving a cheque from a local social club which had organized a fundraising function for the hospice and another local charity (page 144).

The Peggy Nisbet Collectors Reference Book, Silver Jubilee Edition, was published to commemorate the occasion. A supplement was published on 1 January 1979, to bring the range up to date.

The gathering together of so many of my friends and colleagues, all of whom had in some way or another been involved in the Peggy Nisbet Story, was an unforgettable experience, the memory of which will remain with me forever.

Silver Jubilee Reception, November 1977. George Price (London buyer for Triminghams of Bermuda), Peggy Nisbet.

Silver Jubilee Reception, November 1977. British Toy Manufacturers Association. "Tommy" Thomas (editorial), Miss Riley (secretary), John Glanfield (fairs organiser).

Silver Jubilee Reception, November 1977. Basil George of Jersey (far right).

Silver Jubilee Reception, November 1977. Lady Felicity Osborne (niece of Peggy Nisbet) and son.

Silver Jubilee Reception. November 1977. Alison Wilson, Adam and Jennifer Loxton-Peacock (Peggy Nisbet's nephew and wife).

Silver Jubilee Reception, November 1977. R. Pennistone (Selfridges' toy buyer) Malcolm Bowman (Peggy Nisbet Limited), Joy (Selfridges' sales.)

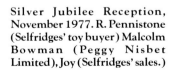

Family Album
—1909-1987—

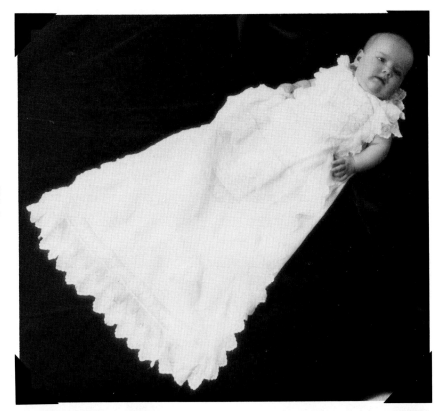

Clementine in her christening
gown, May 1983 (first worn by
her Grandmother, Peggy
Nisbet in 1909).

Michael Fox, Auntie Kitty and Alison.

Auntie Kitty - 1968, age 86.

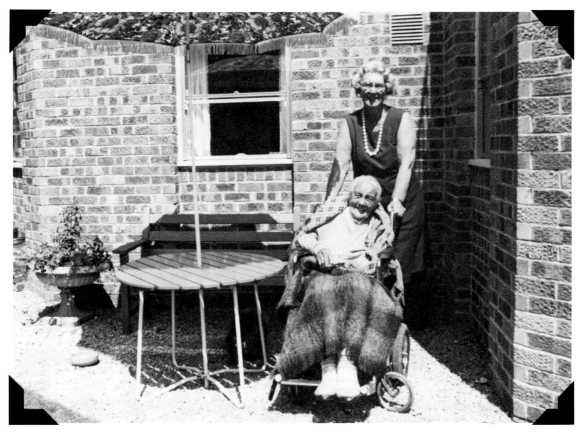

Auntie Kitty in her nineties.

Alison, age 4.

Peggy Nisbet, Peter, Alison and Bill, 1944.

Alison - Medallist Tap Dancing, Bristol Eistedfodd, "Music, Music, Music," 1949.

Alison in Hungarian dress, 1952.

"Defending our House," World War II, Peter, age 5 and troops.

ABOVE LEFT: Peggy Nisbet as "Little Boy Blue," age 11.

ABOVE RIGHT: Peggy Nisbet, age 15.

RIGHT: "On My Wedding Day" 9th June 1934.

Mother, Nancy and Peggy
Nisbet (right).

Family house, Bristol, (where
Peggy Nisbet was born, 1909).

150

Bill and Alison, 1947.

Peter and Mary's wedding. 1958. Bridal doll made with Mary's original dress material.

Jack and Alison's wedding, 9th June 1976.

Epilogue
——1987——

My personal story of the building of the Peggy Nisbet doll-making business brings me up to the early 1980s, by which time Jack and Alison were running the company. I must now bring its history up to date.

During the last few years the company has expanded rapidly under Jack's management. He has grouped together Peggy Nisbet Limited, Childhood Classics and Tower Treasures Limited to form The House of Nisbet Ltd.

Jack is also interested in bears, his close friendship with the late Peter Bull, actor and arctophile inspired the creation of the Bully family of bears, and then the 12 *Zodiac Bears*, which have been so popular. This has been followed by the introduction of an authentic replica of *Delicatessen* (the Bear who played Aloysius in "Brideshead Revisited").

The House of Nisbet Ltd. is now the leading company in the country of collectable bears of high quality and originality. Jack has developed the Nisbet/Doulton bone china bisque dolls, and a range of beautiful wax dolls, both of which are sought after by collectors. He has broken new ground with hand-carved wood and dressed nativity figures; a celebrity collection of bears and a completely new concept *Body Language Bear*.

Alison continues as Designer Director, with Mabel Perry and Brigitte Charsley as her assistants.

Jack was born in Toronto. His first job was with the Toronto Transit Commission; then he joined Letraset, Canada, as General Manager. He was appointed Director of European Operations, then Director of World Operations during which time he was based in the United Kingdom. He attended a three months' Harvard business course in Switzerland, joined Peggy Nisbet Limited in 1974 and married my daughter, Alison, in 1976.

It is just over 30 years since I turned an idea into reality, but conditions are now very different from those in the fifties, and I wonder how I would have fared to-day.

Businesses then were smaller, everything moved at a slower pace, and one could plan well in advance. Buyers at the January fairs would place their main spring, summer and even Christmas orders so one could order materials in advance and prepare a manufacturing schedule. To-day many buyers can only order one month in advance, their budget being controlled not by their own expertise and experience, but by accountants working from computerised sets of figures in some office hundreds of miles away. Companies change hands with monotonous regularity until one does not know with whom one is dealing.

Attitudes, too, have changed. Personal contacts and loyalties have in many cases disappeared, resulting in a lack of enthusiasm and motivation. However, as I finish this book in 1987 there already appears to be a swing back; many men and women who were made redundant by large companies have, with government help, used their redundancy payments to start up small family businesses. They are working hard and enthusiastically and in many cases proving remarkably successful doing work for which they are suited and which they enjoy.

They will find, as I did, that they must keep their promises, plan long term, cultivate good judgment, keep a sense of humour and above all maintain a reputation for integrity in all their dealings. One should lead the market and not follow the ideas of others and not be panicked into wasting time on short term projects because of any temporary slowing down of business.

One has to be enormously resilient to do this but perseverance and a reasonable amount of optimism will bring their rewards.

My advice to anyone who might wish to take it, is to treat others as you would wish to be treated, be honest and fair in your dealings, and above all, never to give up!

Range	Listed Items
H	164
P	167
LE	38
T	108
N	90
BR	86
S	11
F	12
K	27
D	9
P.T.	19
BUDGET	5
BP	11
MIN	19
IL	9
SPECIALS	2
A (VINYLS)	24
WD	6
RAG	18
BDAY	14
NCC	23
	862

Catalogue Listings

Historical Characters - "H" Range

H/200 Anne of Green Gables
H/201 Jacobean Lady
H/202 Elizabethan Lady
H/203 Elizabethan Gent
H/204 Georgian Lady
H/205 Victorian Miss
H/206 Victorian Lady in Bustle
H/207 Georgian Gent
H/208 13th Century Lady
H/209 Mary, Queen of Scots
H/210 Bonnie Prince Charlie
H/211 15th Century Noble Lady
H/212 15th Century Lady
H/213 Norman Queen
H/214 Queen Elizabeth I
H/215 Marie Antoinette
H/216 Lady Jane Grey
H/217 Anne Boleyn
H/218 King Henry VIII
H/219 Katherine of Aragon
H/220 Jane Seymour
H/221 Catherine Howard
H/222 Anne of Cleves
H/223 Catherine Parr
H/224 Flora MacDonald
H/225 Crinoline Lady
H/226 Betsy Ross
H/227 Madame Pompadour
H/228 Empress Josephine
H/229 Napoleon Bonaparte
H/230 Elysabeth of York
H/231 King Henry VII
H/232 Lady Hamilton
H/233 Horatio, Lord Nelson
H/234 Lady Fitzherbert
H/235 The Prince Regent

H/236 Beau Brummel
H/237 Queen Anne
H/238 Queen Margaret (Scotland)
H/239 Henrietta Maria
H/240 Queen Adelaide
H/241 King George II
H/242 Queen Caroline
H/243 Augusta, Princess of Wales
H/244 Duchess of Devonshire
H/245 Mary Livingstone
H/246 Mary Beaton
H/247 Mary Seaton
H/248 Mary Fleming
H/249 Queen Anne of Denmark
H/250 Robin Hood
H/251 Sheriff of Nottingham
H/252 Friar Tuck
H/253 George Washington
H/254 Martha Washington
H/255 Maid Marion
H/256 Margaret of Anjou
H/257 Marguerite De Valois
H/258 Victorian Lady
H/259 Court Lady 1780
H/260 Edwardian Lady
H/261 Hengist
H/262 King Arthur
H/263 Queen Judith
H/264 Queen Guinevere
H/265 Isabella (Edward II)
H/266 Queen Catherine
H/267 King Henry V
H/268 Regency Lady
H/269 Regency Dandy
H/270 King Louis XV
H/271 Madame Du Barry
H/272 Pope John XXIII
H/273 Mary Tudor
H/274 Amy Robsart
H/275 Nell Gwynn
H/276 Lady Harriet
H/277 Miss Amelia
H/278 Mary, Queen of Scots
H/279 Bonnie Prince Charlie
      (Culloden)
H/280 Mary Poppins
H/281 Queen Matilda
H/282 William, the Conqueror
H/283 Queen Berengaria
H/284 King Richard I
H/285 Robert, the Bruce
H/286 Catherine of Braganza
H/287 Lady Castlemaine
H/288 Queen Charlotte Sophia
H/289 Sarah Siddons
H/290 Empress Eugenie
H/291 Dame Ellen Terry
H/292 Lily Langtry
H/293 Queen Eleanor of Portugal
H/294 Queen Marie Theresa
H/295 Catherine, the Great
H/296 Scottish Lady

H/297 King Edward II
H/298 Queen Isabella (Edward II)
H/299 King John
H/300 Queen Isabella (King John)
H/550 Cavaliers Lady
H/551 Gainsborough Lady
H/552 King William III
H/553 Queen Mary II
H/554 King George III
H/555 Queen Charlotte
H/556 Edwardian Lady Motorist
H/557 Edwardian Motorist
H/558 17th Century Lady
H/559 King James IV Scotland
H/560 Scottish Noble Lady
H/561 Cameron of Lochiel
H/562 Fraser Man
H/563 Fraser Lady
H/564 King Louis XIV
H/565 Queen Caroline
H/566 Baron - King John Court
H/567 Baron's Lady
H/568 Pilgrim
H/569 Mid-Victorian Lady
H/570 Princess Charlotte
H/571 King Edward III
H/572 Queen Philippa
H/573 Duchess of Bedford
H/574 Katherine, the Fair
H/575 Duchess of Marlborough
H/576 King Malcolm III
H/577 St. Margaret of Scotland
H/578 Edwardian Boy
H/579 Bride
H/580 Bunratty Castle (Blue)
H/581 Bunratty Castle (Green)
H/582 Bunratty Castle (Violet)
H/583 King Charles VII
H/584 Queen Marie of Anjou
H/585 Joan of Arc
H/586 King Edward I
H/587 Edward - Prince of Wales
H/588 Eleanor of Castile
H/589 Black and White Minstrels (M)
H/590 Black and White Minstrels (F)
H/591 King William IV
H/592 Lady Randolph Churchill
H/593 John Churchill
H/594 Princess Alexandra (Fife)
H/595 President Lincoln
H/596 Jane - Duchess of Gordon
H/597 Princess Alice
H/598 Helen of Troy
H/599 Robert Bruce
H/801 Ascot Lady
H/802 Gibson Girl
H/807 Sir Thomas More
H/808 Duchess of Portsmouth
H/809 Dudley - Earl of Leicester
H/810 Countess of Warwick
H/811 Peeress of the Realm
H/812 Marquis of Montrose

H/813	Princess Beatrice	P/618	Robert Burns	P/709	King George V
H/814	Minute Man	P/619	Bonnie Prince Charlie	P/710	Queen Mary
H/815	Minute Man's Wife	P/620	Flora MacDonald	P/711	King Edward VII
H/816	American Trooper	P/621	Cardinal Wolsey	P/712	King George VI
H/817	Redcoat	P/622	Sir Francis Drake	P/713	Queen Elizabeth
		P/623	Mary Tudor	P/714	Lily Langtry
		P/624	Prince Albert	P/717	John Kennedy
		P/626	Mary Livingston	P/718	Jacqueline Kennedy
		P/627	Mary Beaton	P/725	Franklin Roosevelt

Portrait ("P") Range

P/400	Queen Elizabeth II - State Robes	P/628	Mary Seaton	P/726	Eleanor Roosevelt
P/401	Queen Elizabeth II - Garter Robes	P/629	Mary Fleming	P/727	John Adams
P/402	Prince Charles	P/630	Lord Darnley	P/728	Abigail Adams
P/403	Prince Philip	P/631	James Hepburn	P/729	Benjamin Franklin
P/404	Queen Mother	P/633	Flora MacDonald	P/730	Will Rogers
P/405	Princess Anne	P/635	John Knox	P/731	Theodore Roosevelt
P/406	Queen Elizabeth II - Thistle Robes	P/636	King Edward VI	P/732	Edith Roosevelt
P/408	Queen Elizabeth II Trooping Colour	P/637	Robert Bruce	P/733	Harry S. Truman
		P/638	King James VI and I	P/734	Elizabeth Truman
P/409	Prince Charles - Grenadier Guards	P/639	King Charles II	P/735	Dwight D. Eisenhower
		P/640	Pope John XXIII	P/750	Clark Gable
P/410	Prince Philip - Naval Uniform	P/641	Princess of Wales 1875	P/752	Jean Harlow
P/411	Prince Charles - Robe	P/642	King Henry VI	P/753	Greta Garbo
P/413	Prince Andrew - Balmoral	P/643	Margaret of Anjou	P/754	Judy Garland
P/414	Prince Edward - Balmoral	P/644	King Edward IV	P/755	Charlie Chaplin
P/415	Queen Elizabeth II Jubilee	P/645	Elizabeth Wydeville	P/756	Stan Laurel
P/417	Princess Margaret	P/646	Warwick, the Kingmaker	P/757	Oliver Hardy
P/418	King Edward VIII	P/647	Countess of Warwick	P/758	Elizabeth Taylor
P/419	Mrs. Simpson	P/648	King Richard III	P/759	W. C. Fields
P/421	Princess Elizabeth	P/649	Queen Anne	P/761	Vivien Leigh
P/422	Princess Margaret	P/650		P/763	Danny Kaye
P/423	Prince Charles	(a)	Edward V	P/764	Bob Hope
P/424	Lord Mountbatten	(b)	Duke of York	P/786	Countess of Warwick
P/450	Queen Anne	P/651	King Henry VII	P/787	Hon. Alice Keppel
P/451	Prince George - Denmark	P/652	Queen Elysabeth of York	P/788	Lily Langtry
P/452	Queen Mary II	P/671	Campbell of Argyle	P/789	Princess Victoria
P/453	King William III	P/672	MacDonald of the Isles	P/790	Kaiser Frederick III
P/456	King Richard III	P/673	MacLeods	P/791	Tsaritsa Alexandra
P/457	Anne Nevill	P/674	Stewarts	P/792	Tsar Nicholas II
P/458	King Louis XVI	P/675	Camerons	P/793	Queen Ena of Spain
P/459	Marie Antoinette	P/676	Sinclairs	P/794	King Alfonso XIII
P/460	Napoleon	P/677	Mistress of Robes	P/795	Joan of Arc
P/461	Josephine	P/678	Earl Marshall	P/796	Sir W. Churchill
P/462	Lord Nelson	P/685	Oliver Twist	P/797	Pope John XXIII
P/463	Lady Hamilton	P/686	Artful Dodger	P/798	Capt. James Cook
P/464	Shah of Iran	P/687	Fagin	P/799	Rob Roy
P/465	Empress of Iran	P/688	Bill Sykes	P/800	St. Margaret
P/601	Queen Elizabeth I	P/689	Nancy	P/820	Charlotte Bronte
P/602	Katherine of Aragon	P/690	Mr. Bumble	P/821	Pope John Paul II
P/603	Anne Boleyn	P/691	Queen Elizabeth I (special)	P/822	Margaret Thatcher
P/604	Jane Seymour	P/692	Sir F. Drake (special)	1002	King Tutankhamen
P/605	Anne of Cleves	P/694	Anna of Austria	1003	Queen Nefertiti
P/606	Catherine Howard	P/695	Sir W. Raleigh		
P/607	Catherine Parr	P/696	Napoleon		
P/608	Mary, Queen of Scots	P/697	Josephine	**Limited Edition Models**	
P/609	King Charles I	P/698	Duke of Wellington	LE/50	King Louis XIV
P/610	Queen Victoria	P/699	Duchess of Richmond	LE/51	Queen Marie Thérèse
P/611	King Edward VII	P/700	Duke of Gordon	LE/52	Duchess De La Valliere
P/612	Queen Alexandra	P/701	Queen Victoria	LE/53	Marquise De Montespan
P/613	King George V	P/702	George Washington	LE/54	Madame De Maintenon
P/614	Queen Mary	P/703	Paul Revere	LE/55	Queen Mary I
P/615	Sir W. Churchill	P/705	Indian Warrior	LE/56	King Philip of Spain
P/616	Sir W. Scott	P/706	King George III	LE/57	Queen Katherine of Aragon
P/617	Wm. Shakespeare	P/707	Queen Charlotte	LE/58	M. Plantagenet
		P/708	Queen Victoria - State Robes	LE/59	Dona Elvira
				LE/60	King William IV

LE/61	Queen Adelaide	T/111	David - Welsh Boy	T/178	Jenny - West Country
LE/62	Mrs. Dorothea Jordan	T/112	William - English Boy	T/179	Lucky Pixie
LE/63	Catherine of Oldenburg	T/113	Charlotte - Old English	T/180	Gwennie - Welsh
LE/64	Prince Regent	T/114	Maggie - Scottish Fish Wife	T/181	Girl Piper
LE/65	Queen Caroline	T/115	James - Scots Drummer	T/182	Mary - English Country
LE/66	Princess Charlotte	T/116	Robert - Scottish Chieftain	T/183	Annie - English Fishergirl
LE/67	Mrs. Fitzherbert	T/117	Leslie - Scottish Private	T/184	Patsy - Chorus Girl
LE/68	Countess of Jersey	T/118	Charles - Highland Dress	T/185	Angus - Highland Shepherd
LE/69	King Arthur	T/119	Francis - Eliz. Sea Captain	T/186	Bella - Highland Shepherdess
LE/70	Queen Guinevere	T/120	Robert Burns		
LE/71	Sir Lancelot	T/121	Bruce - Scottish Officer		**National Range**
LE/72	Lady Anne	T/124	English Folk Dancer	N/101	France - Brittany
LE/73	Lady Sybil	T/126	Dolly Vardon	N/102	Hungary
LE/79	King Richard I	T/127	Nun	N/103	France
LE/80	Eleanor of Aquitane	T/128	Morris Man	N/104	Italy
LE/81	Queen Berengaria	T/129	Gwynneth (Welsh Girl)	N/105	France - Riviera
LE/82	Standard Bearer	T/130	Isobel (S.O.B.H.D.)	N/106	France - Alsace
LE/83	King Charles II	T/131	Christmas Fairy	N/107	Switzerland
LE/84	Nell Gwyn	T/132	Gendarme	N/108	Austria
LE/85	Countess of Castlemaine	T/133	Bride	N/109	Holland - Girl
LE/86	Duchess of Portsmouth	T/134	Soldier	N/110	Sweden
LE/88	The Straw Hat (Rubens)	T/135	Cricketer	N/111	Spain - Toreador
LE/89	Mrs. Graham (Gainsborough)	T/136	Footballer	N/112	Spain
LE/90	The Box (Renoir)	T/137	Tennis Girl	N/113	Esthonia
LE/91	K. Henry (Cloth of Gold)	T/138	Jockey	N/114	Norway
LE/92	Catherine of Aragon	T/139	Robin Hood	N/116	Japan
LE/93	Cardinal Wolsey	T/140	Simone - Guernsey Maid	N/117	India
		T/141	Guernsey Maid	N/118	Red Indian Girl
	6in (15cm) Happy Dolls	T/142	French Girl	N/119	China
T/10	Canadian Mountie	T/143	Pilgrim Father	N/120	Can-Can
T/11	Highland Evening Dress	T/144	Pilgrim Mother	N/121	Black Mammy
T/16	Red Cross Nurse	T/145	Germaine - Jersey Maid	N/122	Switzerland (Man)
T/46	Skier	T/146	Cornish Fisherman	N/123	Germany - Black Forest
T/50	Minnie - Parlour Maid	T/147	Cornish Flower Girl	N/124	Germany - Black Forest
T/51	Bobby - London Policeman	T/148	Cornish Fisherwoman		(Male)
T/52	Arthur - Beefeater	T/149	Holland	N/125	Finland
T/53	Jill - Sailor Girl	T/150	Spain	N/126	Denmark
T/60	Wendy - Schoolgirl	T/151	Switzerland	N/127	Iceland
T/62	Jack - Sailor	T/152	Italy	N/128	Portugal
T/63	Scots Dancing Lad	T/153	Austria	N/129	Belgium
T/64	Jock - Scots Piper	T/154	Rebecca - Victorian	N/130	Canada
T/65	John - Guardsman	T/155	Melissa - Regency	N/131	Australian Bushranger
T/67	Nanette - Ballerina	T/156	Jeremy - Regency	N/132	South African Settler
T/71	Margaret - Tartan Dress	T/157	Alexander - MacDonald	N/133	Mexico
T/72	Mairi	T/158	Helen - Murray	N/134	Greece
T/75	Morag	T/159	William	N/135	Greece (Male)
T/76	Bridget - Irish Colleen	T/160	Catherine - Child Bride	N/136	Egypt
T/78	Bronwen - Welsh Girl	T/161	Sarah Jane - Fishwife	N/137	Tyrol
T/80	Elizabeth - English Girl	T/162	Alice - Cream Maker	N/138	Eskimo
T/81	Sally - Holiday Girl	T/163	Fanny - Victorian	N/139	Poland
T/82	Life Boatman	T/164	Gerald - Lifeguard	N/140	Yugoslavia
T/91	Rose - English Girl	T/165	Annie - Dairymaid	N/141	Russian Peasant Girl
T/96	Frou-Frou - Cabaret	T/166	Topsy - Piccaninny	N/142	Germany - Bavaria
T/97	Emily - Victorian Girl	T/167	Gypsy Girl	N/143	Czechoslovakia
T/98	Eskimo Girl	T/168	Scottish Dancer	N/144	Holland - Boy
T/99	Red Indian Girl	T/169	Scottish Dancing Girl	N/145	Russian Cossack
T/100	Elspeth - Scots Dancer	T/170	Scottish Shepherd	N/146	Argentine
T/104	Sonia - Skater	T/171	Cornish Fishwife	N/147	Turkey
T/105	Victoria - Old English	T/172	Highland Mary	N/148	Peru
T/106	Susan - Riding Dress	T/173	White Heather Lass	N/149	Rumania
T/107	George - Marine Drummer	T/174	White Heather Lad	N/150	Sicily
T/108	Violet - Flower Seller	T/175	Canadian Pioneer Miss	N/151	Chile
T/109	Edward - Coldstream Guards	T/176	Scottish Girl Piper	N/152	Pakistan
T/110	Patrick - Irish Boy	T/177	Farmer Giles	N/153	Afghanistan

N/154 Alpine Girl
N/155 Poland - Man
N/156 Alsace Lorraine
N/157 Russian Dancer
N/158 Jamaica
N/159 Indian in Sari
N/160 Jersey
N/161 Afrikaans Flower Seller
N/162 Brazilian Dancer
N/163 Sarah Jane - Fishwife
N/164 Brazil
N/165 S. A. Lekker Meisie
N/166 Kashmir
N/167 Bulgaria
N/168 Morocco
N/169 Esthonia
N/170 Arabia
N/171 Nigeria
N/172 Inca Prince
N/173 Inca Princess
N/174 Bavaria
N/175 Bohemia
N/176 Palestine
N/177 Ukraine
N/178 Ceylon
N/179 N. Z. Maori
N/180 Greenland
N/181 Korea
N/182 Madiera
N/183 Moldavia
N/184 Valencia
N/185 Colombia
N/186 Normandy
N/187 Malta
N/188 Naples
N/189 Luxembourg
N/190 Philippines
N/191 Caribbean

British Traditional Range
BR/301 Wales
BR/302 Ireland
BR/303 Musselburgh Fishwife

BR/304 Lavender Girl
BR/305 Nell Gwyn
BR/306 Cherry Ripe   "Cries
BR/307 Turnips and Carrots   of
BR/308 Strawberries   London"
BR/309 Flower Girl

BR/310 Ireland
BR/311 Scots Lassie
BR/312 Scots Laddie
BR/313 Lord Mayor of London
BR/314 Pearly King
BR/315 Pearly Queen
BR/316 Country Girl
BR/317 Guardsman
BR/318 Cornish Fisherwoman
BR/319 Peeress of the Realm
BR/320 London Policeman
BR/321 Household Cavalry
        (Lifeguards)

BR/322 Household Cavalry
        (The Blues)
BR/323 Modern Highland Dress
        (Lady)
BR/324 Modern Highland Dress
        (Gent)
BR/325 Black Watch Piper
BR/326 Rob Roy
BR/327 Peatgatherer
BR/328 Grenadier Guard
BR/330 Beefeater
BR/331 Sailor
BR/333 London Policeman
BR/339 Scottish Piper
BR/340 Highland Gentlewoman
BR/341 Bonnie Mary
BR/342 Lady in Tweeds
BR/343 Country Gent - Shooting
BR/344 Country Gent - Fishing
BR/345 Country Gent - Hunting
BR/346 Country Gent - Kilt
BR/350 Lady in Tweeds
BR/352 Modern Miss - Party
BR/353 Modern Miss - Tartan
BR/354 Modern Miss - Tartan
BR/355 Quakeress
BR/356 Highland Evening Wear -
        Flora
BR/357 Highland Evening Dress -
        Aboyne
BR/358 Highland Evening Wear -
        Shinrone
BR/360 Tudor Market Woman
BR/361 Dolly Vardon
BR/362 Farmer Giles
BR/363 Morris Dancer
BR/364 Country Dancer
BR/365 English Girl
BR/366 Black Watch Officer
BR/367 Royal Company of Archers
BR/368 Scots Lassie
BR/369 Wales (Cloak)
BR/370 Bride
BR/371 Chelsea Pensioner
BR/372 English Milkmaid
BR/373 Officer - Cameron High-
        landers
BR/374 Lairds Lady
BR/375 Scottish Lady
BR/376 Traditional English Girl
BR/377 Lord Mayor of London
BR/378 Pretty Ribbons
BR/379 Scots Girl - Inverness Cape
BR/380 Tudor Serving Wench
BR/381 Aran Man
BR/382 Scots Girl - Tartan Cape
BR/383 Lady - Clan Ogilvie
BR/385 Southern Belle
BR/386 Colonel - Confederate Army
BR/387 Norman Lady of Court
BR/388 Mediaeval Lady of Court
BR/389 Tudor Lady of Court
BR/390 Elizabethan Lady of Court
BR/391 Stuart Lady of Court

BR/392 Georgian Lady of Court
BR/393 Edwardian Lady of Court
BR/394 Coldstream Guards
BR/395 Highland Lassie
BR/396 Cameron (R. R. McIan)
BR/397 Stewart (R. R. McIan)
BR/398 MacCruimin (R. R. McIan)
BR/399 Lamond (R. R. McIan)

Shakespeare Characters
S/501 MacBeth
S/502 Lady MacBeth
S/503 Romeo
S/504 Juliet
S/505 Falstaff
S/506 Hamlet
S/507 Ophelia
S/508 Bottom
S/509 Anne Hathaway
S/510 Titania
S/511 Oberon

Folk Dancers
F/1 Tarantelle
F/2 Mazurka
F/3 Flamenco
F/4 Ländler
F/5 Gavotte
F/6 English Folk Dancer
F/7 Morris Man
F/8 Scottish Country Dancer (F)
F/9 Scottish Country Dancer (M)
F/10 Irish Jig (F)
F/11 Irish Jig (M)
F/12 Welsh Folk Dancer

Tower Treasures "K" Range
K/1 Guardsman
K/2 Beefeater
K/3 Lifeguards
K/4 Scots Piper
K/5 Gentleman at Arms
K/6 Policeman
K/7 Mountie
K/8 Peigi
K/9 Kirsty - Anderson
K/10 Catriona - Ogilvie
K/11 Bella - Jacobite
K/12 Alison - McDonald
K/13 Eva - Innes
K/14 Jeannie
K/15 Isabel - Tartan Cape
K/16 Fiona - Tartan Dress
K/17 Megan - Welsh Dancer
K/18 Molly - Irish Dancer
K/19 English Girl
K/20 Street Crier
K/21 La Sylphides
K/22 Giselle
K/23 Pilgrim Mother
K/24 Pilgrim Father
K/25 Private - Union Army
K/26 White Heather - Lad
K/27 White Heather - Lass

Tower Treasures "Dumpies"
(Wooden 2½in [6cm])
D/1 England - London
D/2 England - Country
D/3 Scots Piper
D/4 Scotland - Chieftain
D/5 Ireland - Colleen
D/6 Wales
D/7 Guardsman (4in [10cm])
D/8 Piper (4in [10cm])
D/9 Big Chief

Wooden "Peg Tops"
R/1 Miss Muffet
R/3 Jack
R/4 Jill
R/14 Toy Soldier
R/15 Clown
R/19 Red Riding Hood
R/20 Bo-Peep
R/21 Queen of Hearts
R/22 Jester
R/23 Serving Wench
R/24 Mother Hubbard
R/25 Jack Horner
R/26 Polly Flinders
R/27 Simple Simon
R/28 Lavender Blue
R/29 Marjorie Daw
R/30 Curly Locks
R/31 Scottie
R/32 Bimbo

"Budget" Range
B/1 Guardsman
B/2 Piper
B/3 Beefeater
B/4 Pearly Queen
B/5 Lifeguard

"British Pageant" Range
BP/1 Guardsman
BP/2 Policeman
BP/3 Sailor
BP/4 Irish Girl
BP/5 Welsh Girl
BP/6 Scots Boy
BP/7 Scots Girl
BP/8 Scottish Piper
BP/9 Scots Girl
BP/10 Undergraduate Boy
BP/11 Undergraduate Girl

Miniature Range
1in (63cm) to 1ft (31cm)
Historical Series
M/930 K. Henry VIII
M/931 Catherine of Aragon
M/932 Anne Boleyn
M/933 Jane Seymour
M/934 Anne of Cleves
M/935 Catherine Howard
M/936 Catherine Parr

Victorian Collection
M/900 Master of House
M/901 Mistress of House
M/903 Lady Visitor
M/904 Grandfather
M/905 Grandmother
M/907 Maidservant

Williamsburg Collection
M/915 Master of House
M/916 Mistress of House
M/918 Lady Visitor
M/919 Grandfather
M/920 Grandmother
M/922 Maidservant

Specials for Australian Market
Captain Cook
Sir Robert Menzies

New National Range (I.L.)
IL/001 Germany
IL/002 Russia
IL/003 Spain
IL/004 Norway
IL/005 Sweden
IL/006 Denmark
IL/007 Greece
IL/008 Romania
IL/009 Yugoslavia

15in (38cm) Vinyl Dolls
A/1 Denny
A/2 Julie
A/3 Tammy
A/4 Mandy
A/5 Sally
A/6 Felicity
A/7 Katie
A/8 Nancy
A/9 Minnie
A/10 Lucy
A/11 Carrie
A/12 Polly
A/13 Candy
A/14 Dippa
A/15 Debbie
A/16 Pattie
A/17 Emmy
A/18 Lottie
A/19 Lavender Blue
A/20 Mary Mary
A/21 Little Polly Flinders
A/22 Curly Locks
A/23 Betty Blue
A/24 Daffy Down Dilly

Vinyl Walt Disney Characters
WD/1 Christopher Robin & Pooh
WD/2 Piglet, Kanga, Rooh & Eyeore
WD/3 Peter Pan
WD/4 Cinderella
WD/5 Snow White
WD/6 Alice in Wonderland

Rag Dolls - Screen Printed
Freckles 18in (46cm) and
  miniature
Clown 24in (61cm) and
  miniature
Piccaninny 18in (46cm) and
miniature

The Herbs (BBC)
Parsley
Dill
Sage

Pogles Wood (BBC)
Mr. Pogle
Mrs. Pogle
Pippin
Tog

Dick Bruna Characters
Miffy
Eskimo
Jesus
Mary

Know Your Numbers
Know Your Colours

Special Queen Elizabeth II
  Sailor for Conrad Lineıe

Robertson's Golly

Nisbet Victorian Birthday Dolls
Genuine Staffordshire
Fine Bone China Heads
V/850 Monday's Girl
V/851 Monday's Boy
V/852 Tuesday's Girl
V/853 Tuesday's Boy
V/854 Wednesday's Girl
V/855 Wednesday's Boy
V/856 Thursday's Girl
V/857 Thursday's Boy
V/858 Friday's Girl
V/859 Friday's Boy
V/860 Saturday's Girl
V/861 Saturday's Boy
V/862 Sunday's Girl
V/863 Sunday's Boy

Nisbet Childhood Classics
Beatrix Potter Range
5200 Peter Rabbit 15in (38cm)
5204 Tom Kitten 15in (38cm)
5205 Jemima Puddleduck 15in
  (38cm)
5206 Foxy Gentleman 15in (38cm)
5207 Lady Mouse 15in (38cm)
5208 Mrs. Tiggywinkle 15in (38cm)
5210 Benjamin Rabbit 15in (38cm)
5213 Old Mrs. Rabbit 15in (38cm)
5214 Samuel Whiskers 15in (38cm)
5350 Peter Rabbit 8in (20cm)

5351	Tom Kitten 8in (20cm)
5352	Jemima Puddleduck 8in (20cm)
5353	Foxy Gentleman 8in (20cm)
5354	Lady Mouse 8in (20cm)
5355	Mrs. Tiggywinkle 8in (20cm)

Nisbet Teddy Bears

5050	Chestnut 26in (66cm)
5052	Chestnut 13in (33cm)
5060	Golden 26in (66cm)
5051	Golden 17in (43cm)
5070	Champagne 26in (66cm)
5023	Trumper 17in (43cm)
5024	Trumper Mascot 8½in (22cm)
5025	Nisbet Cumbrin Bear

INDEX

A

Adams, Kate (Auntie Kitty), 17, 22, 23, 28, 34, 41, 73, 74, 106, 146, 147
Alford, Sally, 72
Allan, Mr. & Mrs., 34
Allen Family, 33
American Trooper, 94
Anderson, Andrew and Margaret, 45
Andrews, Vic, 55
Anne Boleyn, 38, 60
Anne of Austria, 50
Anne of Cleves, 60
Anne (princess), 7
Arabella Stuart, 13, 98
Argentina, 89
Artful Dodger, 58

B

BEA (British European Airways), 111
BOAC (British Overseas Airways Corporation), 111
B.T.H.A. (British Toys and Hobbies Association), 33, 34, 107
B.T.M.A. (The British Toy Manufacturers' Association), 32, 33, 34, 47, 65, 66, 137, 142
Ballerina, 27
Barbier, Ron, 37, 38
Baron of King John's Court, 62
Baron's Lady, 62
Beefeater, 64, 112
Belly Dancer, 112
Benore, Beth and Mary Beth, 131
Bethnal Green Museum, 125, 133
Bill Sykes, 58
Bird, Sylvia, 31, 39, 41, 72
Black Watch Piper, 64, 93
Bloom, Claire, 112

Body Language Bear, 152
Bowman, Malcolm and Jean, 31, 34, 39, 41, 145
Boy and Girl Dancers, 65
Brewer, Dan, 124
Brighton Toy Fair, 32, 33, 41, 47, 50
British Exhibition, The, 49, 50
British Redcoat, 94
Bruna, Dick, 42, 87, 115
Buchholz, Shirley, 133
Bull, Peter, 152
Bully Bears, 152
Butler, Sir Thomas, 112

C

Cadbury, Betty, 100, 102
Cameron, Ronald, 36, 138, 140
Campbell Tartan, 65
Captain Mark Phillips, 16
Cardinal Wolsey, 61
Carlberg, Mildred and William, 123, 124, 125
Casita, Edyth, 77, 129
Catherine Howard, 60
Catherine of Aragon, 61
Catherine Parr, 60
Chad Valley Co. Limited, The, 83, 85
Charles Edward Stuart, 93
Charles (prince), 7
Charlie Chaplin, 36
Charlie Chaplin, 94
Charsley, Brigitte, 42, 66, 152
Cherry Ripe, 18
Childhood Classics, 113, 152
Christopher Robin, 117
Churchill, Randolph, 50
Churchill, Sir Winston, 50
Coleman, Dorothy, Elizabeth Ann and Jane, 4, 80, 100, 101, 102, 111, 126, 129, 133
Coles, Alec, 121, 123
Cook, Ted, Martha and Gary, 53, 78, 79
Crane, Michael John, 24
Cries of London, The, 18, 19, 58
Crook, Pam, 42
Crown & Andrews Pty Ltd., 55
Crown, Gerry, 55

D

Days of the Week, The, 100
Daytons Hudson Department Stores, 75, 76, 77, 78, 79
Dean's Rag Book Co., 23, 24
de Clifford, Mrs. Nerea, 135
Delicatessen, 152
DeMeane, Cindy, 127
Desmond, Kay, 135
Dickson, Jim, 124
Dill, 87
Doelman, Candace, 133

Doll Club of Great Britain, The, 135
Dollology Club of Washington, 133
Dolls in Revue, 75, 76, 77, 78, 79
Doughty, Mary, 135
Duke of Windsor, 12
Dunkley, Harry, 35, 36, 70

E

Earl Marshall, 141
Eaton, Faith, 100, 101, 111, 135
Edward I, 139
Edward II, 139
Eleanor of Aquitaine, 62
Elizabeth II, 7, 8, 10, 11, 99, 104, 138, 141
Elizabethan Lady, 25
Elizabethan Lady of The Court, 21
Elliott, Richard, 23
Ellis, Dave, 36
Eskimo, 87
Evans, Jane, 121, 123
Eyeore, 117

F

Fagin, 58
Fawdry, Marguerite, 133
Fieldhouse, Bill and Thören, 137
Fisher, Gerry, 53
Fleischman, Mr., 53
Flora MacDonald, 93
Flower Girl, 19, 58
Foire de Lyon, 67
Fox, James, 42
Fox, Michael, 39, 146
Fox, Paula, 77, 78
Foxy Gentleman, 85, 113
France, 89
France-Brittany, 89
Francis, Mary Harris, 131
Friday's Boy, 116

G

Garland, Moira, 135, 136
Garter King of Arms, 4
Gascoigne, Mr., 47, 48
Gentleman Visitor, 88
George, Basil, 142, 143, 144
George V, 8
George VI, 7, 8
Georgian Lady, 25
Gibson, Suzanne, 80
Glanfield, John, 144
Goodfellow, Caroline, 100, 102, 125, 126, 133
Greene, Vivien Graham, 135
Griffin, Brian, 111, 143
Griffith, Ralph, 133
Grove, Elizabeth, 128
Guardsman, 64

H

H.R.H. Princess Margaret, 16
Halberg, Mr. & Mrs., 127
Hall, Gladys, 77
Hall, Joyce, 50
Halpern, Eileen and Mimi, 80, 126, 128
Hamleys, 15, 111, 143
Hancock, Jean, 30, 31, 39, 42, 106, 112
Happy dolls, 19, 31, 65, 118
Harrods, 17, 20, 21, 69, 110
Harrods' Doorman, 91
Healacraft, 99, 100, 116
Heart of England, The, 135
Heidi, 111
Henry VIII, 35, 37, 72
Henry VIII and His Six Wives, 65
Herbs, The, 87, 115
Heritage Award, 77
Hickman, Irene Blair, 135
Highland Chieftains, 65
Hill, Bob and Jean, 80, 126
Hillier, Mary, 100, 102, 121, 135
Hooper, Sylvia, 42, 105
Horn, Howard and Carol, 53
Household Cavalry, 64
Hunt, Mavis, 126, 127
Hunze, Edna, 133

I

Indian Warrior, 94
International Gift Fair, 65, 107
Investiture of The Prince of Wales, 104
Italy, 89
Izal, 112, 119

J

Jack and Jill, 86
Jacqueline Kennedy, 75
Jane Seymour, 60
Jemima Puddleduck, 85, 113
Jetsell, 50, 51
Johnston, Patrick, 8
Josephine Beauharnais, 59
Jubilee Bear, 141
Jubilee Lion, 141
Judy Garland, 94
Juliet, 112

K

Kanga, 117
Katherine of Aragon, 60
Kenyon, Shirley, 69
Kernon, Gillian, 135
King Arthur, 57
King Edward's Chair (coronation chair), 13, 139

King Edward VII, 12
King George V, 12
King George VI, 12
King Henry VIII, 26, 39, 60, 61
King Henry VIII and His Six Wives, 40, 88, 142
King John, 62
King Louis XIV, 59
King of Arms, 13, 138, 141
King Richard I, 62
King Tutankhamen, 90
Knoblauch, Beryl, 133
Knox, John, 126
Kuehn, Ken and Martha, 53, 81, 125

L

Lady Anne, 57
Lady Jane Grey, 13
Lady Mouse, 85, 113
Lady Randolph Churchill, 92
Lady Sybil, 57
Lady Visitor, 88
Lakeland Plangon Club, 135
Lambe, Austin, 53, 54
Lambe, Austin Imports Ltd., 53, 54
Lancaster, Cyril, 8, 17
Lavender Girl, 18, 19, 24, 58
Letitia Penn Doll Club, The, 126
Lewin, John, 24, 27, 139
Locke, Miss, 112, 143
London Policeman, 64
Loosley, John, 103
Lord Chancellor, 15
Lord Chief Justice, 15
Lord Darnley, 93
Loveland, "Pip," 20, 21
Loxton-Peacock, Adam and Jennifer, 145

M

MacDonald, Flora, 103
Macgregor, M.S., 34
Madame de Maintenon, 59
Madame du Barry, 59
Madame Pompadour, 59
Maidservant, 88
Maloney, Mary, 39
Manservant, 88
Mantle, Dorothy, 42
Marchal, Patty, 133
Marchant, Bob, 17, 110
Margaret Thatcher, 36
Marks & Spencer, 83, 84, 85
Marquise de Montespan, 59
Marshall, Barbara, Bob and Barbie-Jo, 50, 52, 131, 134
Marshall Imports, 52
Martha Washington, 75
Martin, Bill and Martha, 80, 81, 116, 126, 130
Mary Lincoln, 75
Mary Poppins, 117

Mary Queen of Scots, 65
Mary Queen of Scots, 13, 22, 72, 93
Mary Tudor, 13
Mayoress, Lady, 112
McAulay, Julie, 22, 23
McBride, Eleanor, 127
McClements, Mrs., 42
McGregor, Michael, 42
Miffy, 87
Milner, Dr. David, 111, 114
Minnetonka Doll and Toy Club, 77
Minter, Mr., 103
Mrs. Tiggywinkle, 113
Miss Muffet, 86
Mr. Bumble, 58
Mistress of the House, 88
Mistress of the Robes, The, 141
Monday's Girl, 116
Mountie, 111
Moynihan, Robert, 53, 78, 79
Murphy, Stan, 143
Musselburgh Fisherwomen, 65

N

N.A.M.E. (National Association of Miniature Enthusiasts), 131
Nancy, 58
Napoleon Bonaparte, 59
National costume dolls, 18, 25
Nefertiti, 37, 90
Nefertiti, 38
Nell Gwyn, Orange Seller, 18, 19
New, Audrey, 55
New York Toy Fair, 33, 65, 107
New Zealand, 89
Nicholson, Mr., 17
Nisbet, Alison (Wilson), 5, 22, 29, 39, 41, 42, 51, 66, 72, 73, 74, 81, 83, 84, 106, 110, 111, 112, 120, 133, 134, 137, 145, 146, 147, 148, 151
Nisbet Childhood Classics, 83
Nisbet, Peter and Mary, 5, 7, 22, 28, 39, 120, 137, 147, 148, 151
Nisbet, William Wood (Bill), 28, 32, 34, 42, 44, 47, 147, 151
Nurnberg Toy Fair, 42, 65, 66, 67, 107

O

Oliver, 58, 110
Oliver Hardy, 94
Oliver Twist, 58
Osborne, Lady Felicity, 145
Over the Rainbow Doll and Toy Club, 77

P

Parsley, 87
Pearly King, 58
Pearly Queen, 58
Pearson, Mr., 8

Peatgatherer, 65
Pedigree Dolls, 84
Peeress of the Realm, 21
Peggy Nisbet, 91, 112, 142
Peggy Nisbet Doll Collectors' Club, 55, 56, 75, 99
Pennistone, R., 145
Perry, John, 68
Perry, Mabel, 34, 41, 42, 68, 73, 74, 79, 104, 106, 110, 111, 112, 114, 152
Peter Rabbit, 113
Philip (prince), 7
Phipps, Karen, 105
Piglet, 117
Pipers, 64, 65, 72
Pippin, 87
Pogle, Mr. & Mrs., 87
Pogles of Pogle Wood, The, 87
Pogles Wood, 115
Poland, 89
Pollock's Toy Shop, 133
Pooh, 117
Poole, Sharon, 121, 123
Pope John Paul, 36, 61
Pope John XIII, 36
Pope John XXIII, 61
Potter, Beatrix, 85, 86, 87, 112, 113, 143
President Reagan, 36
Prestige, Pauline, 21
Price, George, 144
Prime Minister Margaret Thatcher, 92
Prince Albert, 12
Prince Charles, 36
Prince Philip, 13, 14, 15, 36, 138, 140
Princess Anne, 16, 36
Princess Elizabeth, 13
Princess Margaret Rose, 13
Princess Victoria, 16
Purves, Eddie and Isa, 44, 45, 47
Pybus, Keith, 101

Q

Queen Alexandra, 12
Queen Berengaria, 62
Queen Elizabeth, 12
Queen Elizabeth I, 13, 27, 96
Queen Elizabeth II, 7, 8, 13, 14, 15, 36, 37, 69, 138, 139, 140
Queen Elizabeth The Queen Mother, 13
Queen Elizabeth the Queen Mother, 36
Queen Guinievere, 57
Queen Marie Antoinette, 59
Queen Mary, 12
Queen Mary The Queen Mother, 13
Queen's Page, The, 141
Queen Victoria, 12
Queen Victoria, 13, 16, 96, 98, 126

R

Rabey, Dee, 131
Rainford, Mary, 128
Red Riding Hood, 87
Reeves International, Inc., 53, 78, 79
Regency Gentleman, 111
Regency Grandmother, 111
Regency Group, 63
Regency Lady, 111
Riley, Miss, 144
Rintoul, Ian, 48
Robson, "Robbie," 35, 36
Roo, 117
Rosebud, 20, 21
Royal Doulton, 100, 152
Royal Herald, 15, 140, 151
Royal Marine Drummer, 27
Rubin, Phil, 53
Rye, Geoffrey, 103

S

Sage, 87
Sailor, 30, 31, 111
St. Croix Valley Doll and Toy Club, 77
St. Paul Doll and Toy Club, 77
Scotland, 44-48
Scott, Ian Harry, 24
Scottish Dancers, 65
Scottish dolls, 46, 65
Scottish Piper, 27
Selfridges, 20, 21, 145
Shakespeare, 72
Shrubbery Doll Club, 24, 129, 135
Sir Winston Churchill, 92
Slade, Gerda, 22, 23, 41
Smith-Cox, Clifton and Marjorie, 28, 29, 49, 50, 66
Somerset Farmer, 4
South America, 89
Spain, 89
Sproule, Dr. Brian and Irene, 45, 46
Standard Bearer, 62
Stan Laurel, 94
Starkey, Paul, 75, 76, 77
Star of the North Doll Club, 77
Stephens, Cyril, 86, 143
Strawberries Sweet Strawberries, 19
Strawberry Girl, 20
Sussex Doll Club, 135
Sweden, 89
Swinburne-Johnson, Jean and Roger, 83, 137
Switzerland, 89

T

Taylor, Alan and Betty, 99
Teddy Bears, 53, 83, 84, 113
Thatcher, Dennis, 121, 122
Thatcher, Margaret, 33, 105, 121, 122
Thomas, "Tommy," 144

Tog, 87
Tom Kitten, 85
Tom Kitten, 113
Tower Treasures, 11, 31, 51, 98, 108, 152
Tremble, Elizabeth, 78
Turner, Muriel, 73
Turnips & Carrots Ho!, 19, 58
Turrell, Roger, 97, 98, 99, 138
Tutankhamun, 37
Tutankhamun, 38
Twigg, Bettyanne, 80, 133
Twinkle, 111, 119

U

U.F.D.C. (United Federation of Doll Clubs, Inc.), 75, 131-135, 138

V

Victorian Collection, 87, 88

W

Wagstaff, Emily, 27, 47, 73
Warne, Frederick & Co. Ltd., 86
Watt, Jacqueline and Philip, 126, 132, 133
Wellings, Norah, 30
Westlake, Christine, 22, 23, 72
Wheatley, Frederick, 18
Whidbey Island Doll Club, 82
White, Gwen, 100, 101, 135
Wiggin, Jerry, 73
Williams, Mrs., 73
Williamsburg Collection, 75, 88
Wills, Marie, 42, 43
Wilson, Alison (see Nisbet, Alison)
Wilson, Clementine, 146
Wilson, John (Jack), 22, 29, 42, 53, 69, 72, 73, 74, 83, 86, 100, 107, 110, 120, 133, 134, 137, 138, 143, 151, 152
Wiltshire, Graham, 142
Woodspring Museum, 121
Worcester Doll Club, 135
Worlebury, 121
Worthing Museum, 121
Worth, Sue, 8, 73, 74, 75, 100, 106, 138

Y

Yeoman Warder, 64, 112
Yeoman Warder of the Tower of London, 64

Z

Zodiac Bears, 152